Manhunt

Rick L. Singleton

Dedication

This book is dedicated to the men and women who serve faithfully as corrections officers, the most demanding and thankless job in criminal justice.

Acknowledgments

I want to acknowledge the following individuals and organizations that assisted in the apprehension and capture of Casey White and Vicky White.

First and foremost, I thank my Lord and Savior, Jesus Christ, for giving me stamina, wisdom and determination during this most trying time of my career.

Second, I want to thank my family, especially my wife Peggy, for the support they gave me, not just during the eleven days of this event but throughout my career. Law enforcement families are the true unsung heroes of the profession.

I would also like to thank the following individuals, agencies, and units for the work they did in bringing this crisis to a successful end:

- *Investigators with the Lauderdale County Sheriff's Office*
- *Florence Police/Lauderdale County SO Special Operations Team*
- *Agents of the US Marshals Gulf States Regional Fugitive Task Force*
- *Agents of the US Marshals Great Lakes Regional Fugitive Task Force*
- *Sheriff Dave Wedding, Deputies, and Corrections Staff of the Vanderburgh County Sheriff's Office*
- *The Evansville, Indiana Police Department*
- *The tow truck driver in Tennessee*
- *Mr. James Stinson, Evansville, Indiana*
- *The local and national news outlets covered this event and helped us keep getting information out to the public.*

About the Author

Rick Singleton began his law enforcement career in 1972 as a Reserve Deputy Sheriff with the Lauderdale County, Alabama, Sheriff's Office. He was later hired as a corrections deputy at the jail and promoted to Deputy Sheriff in February 1973. After working for the office for approximately five years, he ran for sheriff in 1978, coming in fourth in a twelve-man race.

After the election, he continued his law enforcement career with the Florence, Alabama Police Department, where he rose through the ranks to become the city's police chief in 1996, a position he held until his retirement in 2012. He ran for sheriff again in 2014 and was elected by an overwhelming margin, becoming the county's first Republican sheriff. He was also the only sheriff in the county's history to run unopposed when he ran for re-election in 2018. He retired in 2023, ending a law enforcement career that spans fifty years.

Table of Contents

Preface

On April 29th 2022, at 9:41 a.m., Vicky White, the Assistant Administrator and sixteen-year veteran of the Lauderdale County Detention Center in Lauderdale County, Alabama, walked Casey White (no relation), a convicted felon serving 75 years with the Alabama Department of Corrections and awaiting trial on a capital murder charge in the death of Connie Ridgeway, out the detention center door. A model employee with an unblemished record, the escape caught her supervisors, co-workers, and even her own family totally off guard.

On the run for eleven days, the escape caught the attention of the national media and, ultimately, by media outlets around the world. With a six-hour lead and nothing to go on, the Lauderdale County Sheriff's Office and the United States Marshals Service Gulf States Regional Fugitive Task Force sprang into action. The couple were captured on May 9th in Evansville, Indiana. Vicky White died the next day, the result of a self-inflicted gunshot wound to the head that happened when they were stopped by law enforcement.

This is the story of the escape as shared by Lauderdale County Sheriff Rick Singleton, the man responsible for seeing that Casey White was recaptured and that Vicky White was returned to Alabama to face the consequences of her actions. At the first press conference with the national media, Sheriff Singleton told reporters, "It's all on the table, the good, the bad, and the ugly". He honored that commitment by being accessible and transparent with the media, who he credits with playing a major role in apprehending the pair due to the massive coverage they gave the case between April 29th and May 9th.

Lauderdale County Alabama Sheriff Rick Singleton (retired)

Official portrait of Assistant Director of Corrections Vicky White (Photo courtesy of Lauderdale County Sheriff's Office)

CHAPTER 1

Vicky White: A Model Employee

Vicky, seen with friend and co-worker Christina Keeton, on her first time flying to attend a training conference in Denver, Colorado. (Photo by Rick Singleton)

Vicky (Davis) White was a quiet, private person born and raised in Center Hill, Alabama, a small community in Northeast Lauderdale County. She attended T. M. Rogers High School and married Tommy White in 2002. The marriage lasted only 4 years, with the pair divorcing in 2006 as a result of Tommy's alcohol and drug use, something Vicky would not tolerate. They had no children. Tommy died in January 2022 of complications from Parkinson's Disease. Although divorced, Vicky remained friends with Tommy and his mother. Vicky didn't begin her career with the Lauderdale County Sheriff's Office until after her divorce from Tommy. Having passed away just a few months before the escape, at first there was speculation that his death may have been a factor in Vicky's decision to risk everything to help Casey escape, but as it turned out, she and Casey began a relationship soon after his first stay at the Lauderdale County Detention Center in 2020, nearly two years earlier.

Vicky receives her first Employee or Supervisor of the Year award from Sheriff Singleton in 2015. She received the award a total of four times over seven years. She had been voted to receive it a fifth time in 2022.
(Courtesy of LCSO)

An employee's work ethic says a lot about them, and whether or not they can be depended on to get the job done. It's a key factor in predicting an employee's overall job performance because it is usually accompanied by other positive attributes such as trust and dependability. You just don't have the same feelings about an employee who is lazy. Vicky White had the kind of work ethic employers like to see in their employees.

The Lauderdale County Detention Center was Vicky's life. She began her career in 2005 as a corrections deputy and was later promoted to sergeant. When I took office in 2015, I reorganized the rank structure in the detention center assigning two assistant directors, one over operations and the other over administration. Vicky was a natural for the operations side of the house. She knew the detention center, the policies, and requirements of the job, how to manage the staff and inmates like the back of her hand. She had developed the complete trust and confidence of her peers and co-workers and was respected by everyone who worked around her.

Perhaps one of the best measures of that respect is when your peers nominate you for the most prestigious annual award that can be bestowed on someone, Employee or Supervisor of the Year. Vicky got that award four years out of seven and was due to receive it for a fifth time in 2022. That's why the events of April 29th, 2022, came as a complete shock to all of us who worked with her. From her subordinates at the detention center, deputies, supervisors, and clerical employees at the sheriff's office, the district attorney's office, judges, and myself. We didn't know the Vicky White we saw that day.

Vicky White explains housing issues with local media. (Photo by Dan Busey/Times Daily)

Photo of Vicky White along with newspaper articles concerning her work and awards. (Used with permission WAAY 31 News)

Vicky was the go-to person at the Detention Center. If you needed anything you could count on her to take care of it. She had NEVER done anything to give any of us reason not to trust her. One of the judges said, "If you lined ten corrections officers against the wall and told me one of them was going to do this (assist an inmate escape) she would have been number 10 on my list." We felt the same way. We were in total disbelief and denial those first few hours. Vicky would not do this (help an inmate escape). Those first few hours, my head was telling me there was more going on than we realized, but my heart just didn't want to believe it. There was just no way Vicky would participate in such a scheme voluntarily, or so

I wanted to believe. And then we saw the video of her leading Casey out of the DC in violation of policy and protocols. We also learned she had lied to her coworkers about the scheduled court appearance, Vicky had been working there for sixteen years and had an unblemished record, so why would she do that? We would

Vicky with two of her best friends, Deputy Christina Keeton who started her career at the Detention Center, and Judge Carole Medley, whose courtroom Vicky spent a lot of time in. (Lauderdale County Sheriff's Office).

have never questioned anything she said. We had no reason to question her. There HAD to be an explanation, and there could only be one reason: Casey claimed he had been hired to kill Connie Ridgeway, yet he never gave up a name. If that were the case, then that person must have gotten to Vicky, threatened and/or coerced her or her family, forcing her to break him out in fear of his/her name coming up.   As the hours and days passed, it became crystal clear that Vicky was very much involved in planning and executing the plan to get Casey White out of jail, totally against her character and certainly not the Vicky White I, and everyone who worked with and around her, knew.

Vicky was often in the courthouse escorting inmates to court as seen in this photo.
(Photo by Dan Busey/Times Daily)

Casey White's 2015 Mug Shot (Limestone County Sheriff's

CHAPTER 2

Who Is Casey White?

Casey White was born August 20, 1983. While we don't know if he had run-ins with the law as a juvenile, although my guess is he did, we do know that he is a career criminal with an extensive criminal history dating back to 2003 when he was nineteen years old. That criminal history ranges from charges of public intoxication to capital murder.

Photo of woman's vehicle that Casey shot into while trying to hijack it at a rest stop in Giles County, Tennessee. She was hit but survived. (Giles County Sheriff's Office, Tennessee)

In January of 2003, Casey was charged with several offenses related to an apparent vehicle pursuit in Minor Hill, a small community just across the Alabama State Line in Giles County, Tennessee. He was convicted and served 31 days in the Giles County Jail as a result of those charges. Over the years, he was charged with numerous offenses including domestic violence, criminal mischief, harassment, and public intoxication. He was charged in 2006 with domestic violence involving an assault on his own mother and again in 2010 when he assaulted his stepbrother with an axe handle. He plead guilty to that charge and was sentenced to six years in prison.

In 2015, Casey went on a "crime spree" that resulted in charges of burglary, robbery, theft, kidnapping, cruelty to animals, attempting to elude, and attempted murder. He broke into his ex-girlfriend's home, held her and her two roommate's hostage, and shot at them as they were fleeing from the house. He killed her dog and then stole

On the scene when Casey White surrendered to Sheriff Mike Blakely of Limestone County, Alabama in 2015. (Limestone County Sheriff's Office)

a vehicle and drove it to a rest stop in Giles County, Tennessee, where he attempted to hijack a semi-truck at gun point. The driver drove off as Casey opened fire. He then shot a woman while attempting to hijack her vehicle. Thankfully, she survived her injuries. After those two attempts, he was successful in hijacking a vehicle from a man at gunpoint and, after firing at the officers, led law enforcement on a chase.

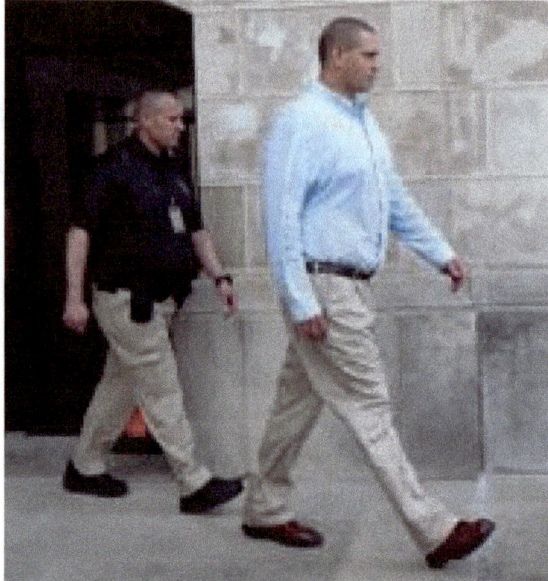

A Limestone County Deputy escorts Casey White from the courthouse during the 2019 trial on charges related to his crime spree in 2015. (WAAY TV)

Casey Whites mugshot from his arrest in 2015 in Limestone County, Alabama. (Limestone County Sheriff's Office)

News coverage of law enforcement in Limestone County re-opening the investigation of Casey White's girlfriend's death in 2008. (WAAY TV)

The pursuit ended in Limestone County, Alabama, with him surrendering to Sheriff Mike Blakely.

Casey White finally got his day in court in June 2019. It had been over three years since his crime spree in Limestone County Alabama and Giles County Tennessee that resulted in his conviction of nine felony charges including one count of attempted murder, two counts for kidnapping, one count of robbery, one count of burglary, one count of cruelty to animals, and one count of breaking and entering a vehicle. The prosecutor in the case praised the witnesses who came forward to testify after experiencing such a traumatic event.

After his escape in 2022 from the LCDC, authorities in Limestone County reopened a case involving a former girlfriend that happened on February 1, 2008. The girlfriend was shot in the chest with a sawed-off shotgun, and her death was ruled a suicide. Casey White was in the home at the time of her death, and her family has always questioned the cause of death. His stepbrother was also reported missing in Lawrence County Alabama, in 2017 and has not been seen or heard from since. The missing persons case is still open.

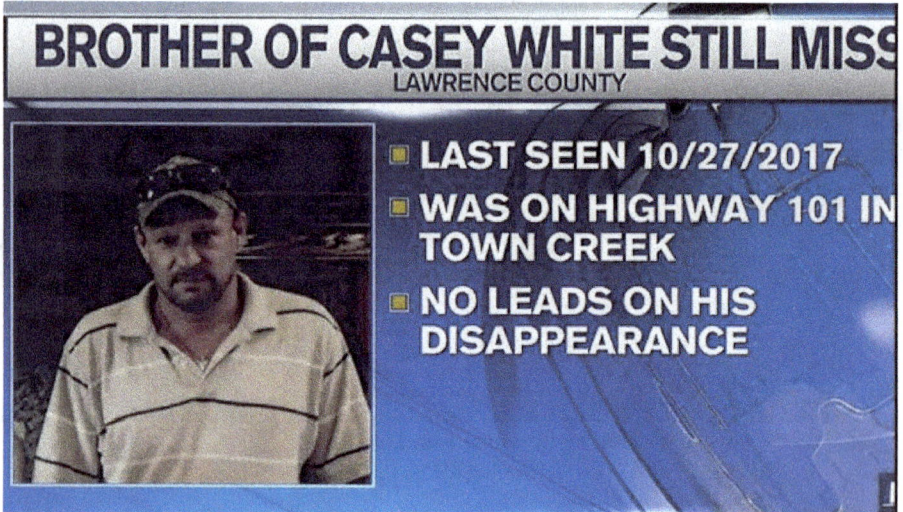

News coverage of Casey Whites missing brother. (WHNT TV)

Name: WHITE, CASEY COLE Jacket #: 19488-1

Booking #: 15728		Book Date: 1/25/2003 2:06:00 PM	Release Date: 1/25/2003 5:00:00 PM	Days: 1
Case No:				
Counts: 1	39-16-603 (	) - EVADING ARREST		
Counts: 1	39-13-103 (	) - RECKLESS ENDANGERMENT		
Counts: 1	39-13-103 (	) - RECKLESS ENDANGERMENT		
Counts: 1	55-10-205 (	) - RECKLESS DRIVING		
Counts: 1	55-9-402 (	) - NO TAIL OR BRAKE LIGHTS		
Booking #: 15912		Book Date: 3/3/2003 8:04:00 AM	Release Date: 4/2/2003 8:04:00 AM	Days: 31
Case No: 49522				
Counts: 1	999 (	) - SERVING TIME ON MITTIMUS		
Booking #: 19210		Book Date: 10/17/2004 3:14:00 AM	Release Date: 10/17/2004 2:00:00 PM	Days: 1
Case No:				
Counts: 1	39-13-103 (	) - RECKLESS ENDANGERMENT		
Counts: 1	55-10-406 (	) - VIOLATION IMPLIED CONSENT LAW		
Counts: 1	55-10-401 (	) - DRIVING UNDER INFLUENCE		
Counts: 1	55-10-104 (	) - DUTY UPON STRIKING UNATTENDED VEHICLE		
Booking #: 19488		Book Date: 12/9/2004 12:35:00 PM	Release Date: 12/10/2004 10:30:00 PM	Days: 2
Case No: 54880				
Counts: 1	999 (	) - SERVING TIME ON MITTIMUS		

Total Charges:

Casey's RAP Sheet from Giles County, Tennessee. (Giles County Sheriff's Office)

Casey White's tattoo's, photos of which were released to aid in identifying him
if spotted.
(Alabama Department of Corrections)

The many faces of Casey White from various mugshots taken during the course
of his criminal career.
(Courtesy of various law enforcement agencies)

Record of Arrest Limestone County Sheriff's Department Athens, Alabama

Name: WHITE, CASEY COLE	Alias:				Our No: 38264		
Address: 808 W PRYOR ST					FBI No:		
City: ATHENS		State: AL	Zip: 35611		SID No:		
Phone: 256-233-4818					SS#: 423-23-8153		
Hgt: 606	Wgt:260	Hair: Brown	Race: White	Sex: M ☒ F☐	DL#: 6964412		
Eyes: Hazel		Complexion: M	DOB: 9-20-83				

Date:	Charge	Officer	FOR	Disposition
9-20-05	RE	M TUCKER	LCSO	9-20-05 EMS
2-19-06	DV 3ᴿᴰ (HARASSMENT)	T CRAIG	LCSO	2-20-06 BOND
3-19-06	CRIMINAL MISCHIEF 3RD	M GUNTER	LCSO	3-19-06 BOND
1/13/08	ASSAULT 3	FLANAGAN	LCSO	1/13/08 BOND
2/3/08	PI	SIMMONS	LCSO	2/16/08 BOND
2/6/08	BOND REV ASSAULT 3	HEAD	LCSO	2/16/08 BOND
10/12/08	RE	STINNETT	LCSO	10/13/08 BOND
9/25/10	DV ASSAULT 2	MCLAUGHLIN	LCSO	9/25/10 BOND
11/28/11	2 CTS DWS, IMP LANE USE, OPEN CONTAINER (ALL ALIAS LAUDERDALE CO)	LEWTER	LCSO	10/24/12 DOC
11/28/11	DV3 HARASSMENT	LEWTER	LCSO	11/28/11 BOND
11/28/11	DV3 HARASSMENT SURETY OFF	RUPP	LCSO	10/24/12 DOC
11/30/11	BOND REV DV2	RYAN	LCSO	10/24/12 DOC
6/10/14	PI	MCNATT	LCSO	6/11/14 BOND
11/21/15	PI	CRAIG	LCSO	11/24/15 BOND
11/24/15	CRIM MIS 3	BROOKS	LCSO	11/24/15 BOND
12/2/15	ATT ELUDE	BLOODWORTH	LCSO	
12/2/15	2 CTS BURG 1; ROBBERY 1; THEFT 1	BLAKELY	LCSO	4/1/16 GJI
12/2/15	ATT COMM MURDER; 3 CTS KIDNAPPING 1; BURG 3; CRUELTY TO ANIMALS	RAMSEY	LCSO	4/1/16 GJI
12/7/15	B&E VEH; PROB VIO ASSAULT 2	RAMSEY	LCSO	
12/7/15	BOND REV CRIM MIS 3	SIMMONS	LCSO	5/25/16 DISMISSED
4/1/16	ATT COMMIT MURDER; 2 CTS BURG 1; 6 CTS KIDNAPPING 1; ROBBERY 1; THEFT 1; BURG 3; B&E VEH; ATT ELUDE; CRUELTY TO ANIMALS GJI	KING	LCSO	6/14/19 DOC

Casey's RAP Sheet from Limestone County, Alabama. (Limestone County Sheriff's Office)

Law enforcement vehicles on the scene at Meadowland Apartments the night Connie Ridgeway's body was discovered by a neighbor. (WAAY TV)

CHAPTER 3

The Murder of Connie Ridgeway

Friday night football is a big deal in Alabama, and the small town of Rogersville turns out in droves to support their Lauderdale County High School (LCHS) Tigers. The stadium was full on October 23rd, 2015, as fans watched LCHS defeat Clements High School, located just across Elk River in Limestone County, by a score of 61 to 0. However, all the excitement wasn't inside the stadium that night. Just across the road, at the Meadowland Apartments, Connie Ridgeway's body had been discovered on the floor of her apartment. She had been brutally murdered, an event that shook the small town to its core.

Connie Ridgeway (Courtesy of Family)

Connie was known as a friendly lady who was always willing to help others. Driving them to appointments, checking on them to make sure they were okay, even trying to rescue a neighbor whose apartment had caught fire. She grew up in Eastern Lauderdale County and attended Lexington High School. A single mother of two young men, Cameron and Austin, she eventually ended up in Rogersville, Alabama, a town of approximately 1,500 situated about half-way between Florence and Athens.

When the call came in that her body had been found in her apartment, the Rogersville Police Department responded, as did the Lauderdale County Sheriff's Office. I responded as well. Officers and investigators from the sheriff's office began to canvas the area and process the crime scene. Being a football weekend, the Rogersville Chief of Police was out of town in Tuscaloosa for the Alabama game the following day. When contacted by his officers and informed of the murder, he instructed them to call the State Bureau of Investigation (SBI) to lead the investigation. Typically, the sheriff's office would assist in such cases but, as the agency of jurisdiction it was the chief's prerogative and responsibility to ask for assistance, if he wanted it, from whomever he wanted. Since the investigation was turned over to the state, our investigators waited on their arrival, briefed the state investigators on what they had done up to that point, and offered their assistance. The State took over the crime scene, and county investigators left. Just a few weeks later the lead investigator with the SBI left for the Middle East on a one-year deployment with the National Guard. As a result, the case hit a stalemate. With little being done, frustration began to build with Connie's family and close friends who were pushing for the case to be solved. I received several calls from Mark White, a former police officer and friend of the family, asking for our involvement in the investigation. Not wanting to "step on the toes" of our brothers in blue, the Rogersville Police Department, and the SBI, I resisted but

told him we were more than willing to assist if the State requested our help. As time drug on, and Mark continued to plea on the family's behalf, I announced that we would be actively participating in the investigation at the family's request. Lt. Brad Potts contacted the State investigator, and a meeting was set up to discuss the status of the investigation.

Austin and Cameron Williams pose with the mother, Connie Ridgeway, for a family photo.
(Photo courtesy of Austin and Cameron Williams)

Lt. Brad Potts (Lauderdale County Sheriff's Office)

November 18, 2015

Austin and Cameron Williams

███████████

███████████

Dear Austin and Cameron,

I received your letter dated November 14th concerning the investigation into your mother's death. Let me again express my personal condolences to both of you over the loss of your mom.

I met today with SBI investigator ████████ and discussed your desire for us to get directly involved in the investigation. Just so you know, Investigator ████ has solicited information from some of our officers during the course of his investigation, however, as of today, Lt. Brad Potts will be working directly with him as they try to identify the person or persons responsible for your mother's death and bring them to justice. Due to decisions that were made early on in this investigation, we have a real challenge in front of us and what we are able to do will depend heavily on the support and cooperation of the SBI. Obviously, our only motive is to accommodate your wishes and identify those responsible.

If there is anything else the Lauderdale County Sheriff's Office can do to assist either of you, please do not hesitate to contact us. Lt. Potts phone number is 256-████████ and my number is 256-████████.

Respectfully,

Rick L. Singleton

Rick L. Singleton

Sheriff

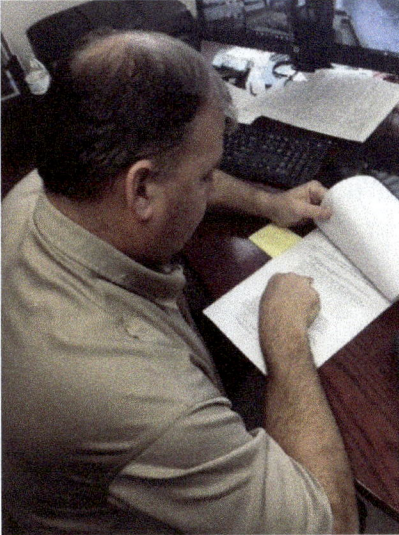

Lt. Brad Potts
(Lauderdale County Sheriff's Office)

Years drug on, and no real leads developed. Lt. Potts was not getting the best cooperation from the State and was severely limited as to what he could actually do given it was not technically our case. But he persisted none-the-less. That persistence eventually paid off. In June of 2020, Lt. Potts received a letter from Casey White, who wanted to talk to him about the murder. Casey White was already serving 75 years on convictions from Limestone County for the string of crimes that he committed there in 2015.

Lt. Potts drove to Donaldson Prison to speak with Casey White about the murder of Connie Ridgeway. During the interview, Casey

Aerial View of Donaldson Correctional Facility. (Alabama Department of Corrections)

confessed to her murder. Once Potts had the case file ready, District Attorney Chris Connolly presented it to the Grand Jury, and Casey White was indicted on two charges of Capital Murder. Finally, there was a degree of closure for the family, but there was still a major question lingering.

White, in his statement, said he was paid by a third party to commit the murder, a statement that would cause concern on April 29th as to a possible motive for Vicky White helping him escape.

Entrance to Donaldson Correctional Facility in Bessemer, Alabama.
(Alabama Department of Corrections)

Local media reports the arrest of Casey White in the Connie Ridgeway murder.
(With permission of WAFF 48, Huntsville, AL)

CHAPTER 4

The Confession

It had been four years since the murder of Connie Ridgeway and, although there had been leads and information over that time, there was still no one charged with her murder. Lt. Potts received several calls himself concerning the case, and followed up on every lead, but still nothing had materialized. With the state investigator out on military duty for a year, and us with very limited access to his file, the case had virtually gone nowhere.

Not surprisingly, the State Bureau of Investigation (SBI) wanted all the information we were able to develop, but getting them to share what they had with us was a real challenge. After all, it was their case, not ours. And we understood that, but it was frustrating for us nonetheless. We were reminded every year during a memorial service held in Connie's memory that the murderer was still out there, and we all wanted them caught. In cases like this, the longer it drags on the more difficult it becomes to solve. Each year in speaking to the family and friends of Connie, I wanted to give them hope. It's easy to eventually give up, but they never did. Mark White, a good friend to Austin and Cameron, made sure through the memorial services that the community, and law enforcement, remembered and pushed forward in holding the person or persons responsible for their actions.

Cameron and Austin Williams join District Attorney Chris Connolly and Lt. Brad Potts of the LSCO at a press conference announcing the indictment of Casey Cole White for the murder of Connie Ridgeway.
(Used with permission of WHNT TV))

There had been a couple of suspects identified who investigators thought might be responsible for Connie's death, but so far there was no hard evidence connecting either to the crime scene. Then one day in June 2020, Lt. Brad Potts got a letter from an inmate at Donaldson Correctional Facility in Bessemer, Alabama. That inmate was Casey Cole White whose name was one of the suspects in the case. In the letter, he told Lt. Potts that he wanted to talk to him, and only him, about a homicide case in Lauderdale County. Lt. Potts made the two-hour drive to Bessemer and met with Casey. After a lengthy interview, Potts returned with a confession. Casey White admitted that it was he who had killed Connie Ridgeway, but he added he was hired to do it.

Local media reports the arrest of Casey White in the Connie Ridgeway murder.
(With permission of WAFF 48, Huntsville, AL)

The week after Connie Ridgeways murder, she was to testify as a witness for the prosecution in another case in Lauderdale County. That certainly presented a motive for Casey White's claim that he was a hired gun, but he wouldn't give up a name, and there was never any evidence to substantiate that claim.

The evidence was presented to the Lauderdale County Grand Jury, and they indicted Casey White on two counts of murder in the death of Connie Ridgeway. He was officially charged on August 3rd, 2020. At last there was some closure for the Williams brothers, and the community was able to beathe a sigh of relief. Her killer had finally been identified and arrested.

Austin and Cameron at a memorial service for their mother, Connie Ridgeway.
(East Lauderdale News)

Lauderdale County Detention Center (Photo by Rick Singleton)

CHAPTER 5

A Foiled Escape

Casey White was serving 75 years in the Alabama Department of Corrections for the crimes he committed in 2015 in Limestone County. After meeting with Lt. Potts in June of 2020 he was brought to the LCDC where he continued to be interviewed about the Ridgeway murder. His case went before the grand jury, and on August 3rd he was charged with murder. Now that he had been arrested for the murder of Connie Ridgeway in Lauderdale County he would have to go before the judge for his advisement. That meant meetings with his attorney and appearing before the judge for an advisement and later a plea hearing, therefore he remained in the Lauderdale County Detention Center from August 3, 2020, until November 4th when he appeared in court for his last scheduled hearing before the case was set for trial.

Before he was transported to the courthouse for his hearing on November 4th, investigators received word that he was planning an escape. His plan was to take a corrections deputy hostage using a shank (homemade prison knife). When deputies searched him and his cell, they found two shanks. Given the report of his planned escape, corroborated by finding the shanks, the district attorney, at our request, asked the judge to have him immediately returned to the department of corrections. When he left the courtroom, he was transported directly back to Donaldson Correctional Facility.

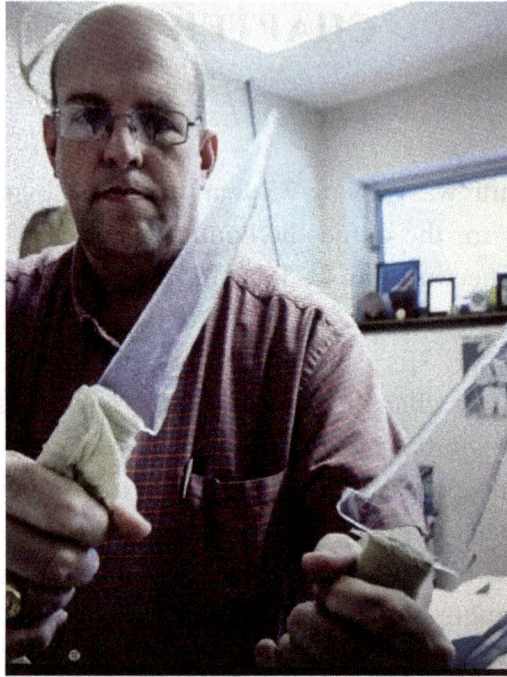

Director Jason Butler shows jail "shanks" recovered from inmates at the LCDC.
(Photo by Dan Busey/Times Daily)

After his return to Donaldson, his court-appointed attorney, who was from Florence, began having issues with DOC concerning access to his client while in prison. He wasn't allowed to bring equipment that he needed to prepare Casey's defense into the prison due to its maximum-security classification. He appealed to the court to have Casey brought back to the Lauderdale County Detention Center so he could have adequate access to his client, and that request was granted. The administration in the sheriff's office was notified of the court order, and the staff at the detention center was reminded of the change in policy that was put in place after the planned escape the previous Fall. At that time, all local transports were being handled by corrections deputies assigned to the DC. After the foiled escape the previous November, that policy was updated in January 2021 to require "sworn" deputies to escort all murder suspects. Based on the court order, Casey White was returned to the LCDC on March 5, 2021.

After preparing his client for trial, Casey White entered a plea of "not guilty" to the charge of murder, and a trial date was set for June 2022. After his plea, he was again returned to Donaldson to await his trial date.

Lauderdale County Sheriff's Office

Law Enforcement

Policies and Procedures

Subject: Transporting Arrested Persons/Inmates	**Policy Number:** **OPS005** (SO080515)
Issue Date: **August 7, 2015**	**Revision Date: January 2021**
Approval *Authority* *Title and Signature:* Sheriff Rick Singleton	

1.   Transport of detainees, for any reason after incarceration, is accomplished by sworn deputies, specially trained corrections deputies, and/or other authorized staff. Transports outside the immediate area require a minimum of two (2) deputies unless otherwise authorized by a supervisor.
2.   Detainees may not be left unattended during transport.
3.   Inmate workers are generally excluded from these procedures unless being transported to court.
4.   No detainee, including inmate workers, will be allowed to smoke or make phone calls, nor are LCSO personnel allowed to make calls on their behalf, while in custody of LCSO.
5.   All inmates charged with any murder related charge are to be escorted by Deputy Sheriff's.

The transport policy at the Lauderdale County Detention Center was amended after the attempted escape of Casey White in 2020. Above is an excerpt from that policy as amended in January 2021. (Lauderdale County Sheriff's Office)

1. Love Behind Bars — and Beyond: How 5 Women Helped Their Lovers Escape Prison

Love Behind Bars — and

Beyond: How 5 Women

Helped Their Lovers Escape Prison

CHAPTER 6

A "Special" Relationship

By Saturday, June 30th, pieces of the puzzle as to what happened in terms of how the escape went down were falling into place. There were three possible scenarios: (1) Casey White somehow overpowered AD Vicky White, took her hostage, and commandeered the patrol car; (2) Someone from outside the facility had gotten to AD White and threatened her or otherwise coerced her into assisting him escape; or (3) Vicky White was a willing participant in the plan.

It was now evident that Casey White did not have time to overpower her and commandeer the vehicle. The short drive to the courthouse takes less than five minutes, and both the detention center and courthouse are in downtown Florence, with heavy traffic and high visibility. It would be virtually impossible for that to happen in such a short time, especially without someone seeing them and reporting it to 911. Besides, by now, we knew the patrol car was captured on a video surveillance camera from a gas station just eight minutes after leaving the detention center, indicating the pair drove directly to the Florence Square Shopping Center where the patrol car was found.

Vicky's patrol vehicle captured on video just eight minutes after leaving the detention center with Casey White. (Lauderdale County Sheriff's Office)

While we wanted to believe that, somehow, Vicky was coerced into assisting Casey escape, there was absolutely no evidence we could find to support that theory. That only left one option; Vicky was in on the escape plan and voluntarily participated, a fact that was extremely difficult for any of us who knew and worked with her to fathom.

The Saturday after the escape, we learned from inmates that Vicky and Casey had, as they described it, a "special" relationship while he was incarcerated in the LCDC in 2021. They said she would see that he got extra food, would get him cigarettes and other items that were prohibited by policy. During the course of the investigation, we found out that relationship continued after he was returned to Donaldson. We soon discovered they had maintained contact via phone calls and that Vicky had been putting money in his commissary account. In fact, we later learned that they began talking by telephone after he was returned to Donaldson Prison in November 2020. Those calls continued and intensified after his second incarceration at LCDC, with a total of 959 calls between the two from August 2021 until his return to the LCDC on February 25,

2022. Based on those phone calls, we had no doubt that there had been a physical relationship between the two of them as well.

Jailhouse romances are nothing new. We have all seen them play out many times over the years. In fact, the week after Vicky and Casey walked away from the LCDC, a young woman working at a juvenile detention center in Louisiana helped three young men escape. It has happened before, and it will happen again. The question those of us who worked with Vicky kept asking was, "How in the world did Vicky fall for this guy?" This was certainly NOT the Vicky White we knew and worked with. As a sixteen-year veteran corrections officer who had seen this play out several times over her career, she knew how inmates would manipulate officers. She also knew how these situations always end, with the inmates getting caught or worse. Why would she throw her career, her life, away for a man serving a seventy-five-year sentence and facing charges for capital murder? There indeed had to be very special feelings she developed for Casey for her to do such a thing.

The control room at the Lauderdale County Detention Center. (Photo by Dan Busey/Times Daily)

CHAPTER 7

Casey Returns to the LCDC

Casey's trial date was approaching, and there were pretrial motions scheduled for court proceedings leading up to the trial. For that reason, he was brought back to the Lauderdale County Detention Center on February 25th, 2022. During the investigation into the escape, it was discovered that Vicky, who was also responsible for classification and assigning inmates to specific cells, had Casey assigned to cell block A-1, the first cell block as you enter A Hall. This cell is somewhat secluded from view of other cell blocks, with the inmate property room being directly across the hall, therefore anything going on in cellblock A1 was out of view of other inmates.

A person charged with capital murder would normally be in a cell by themselves, but that was not an option. Due to the design of the jail, coupled with an ongoing crowding issue, there was no way to isolate him from other inmates. This was another way Vicky was giving him "special" attention. She controlled which inmates, and how many, were in the cell with him. Given his stature, and with Vicky's obvious backing, the few inmates in the cell with him were afraid to talk. In fact, some were reluctant to talk even with him gone in fear he would eventually be returned and would find out.

Casey White was assigned to Cell Block A-1 while in the LCDC. (Lauderdale County Sheriff's Office)

We also found out that Casey and Vicky would exchange notes through the pan-hole in the cell which, in and of itself, was not that unusual. Inmates often pass notes to corrections officers asking them to check into something for them or asking to see a nurse, etc. We don't know what information Casey and Vicky were exchanging

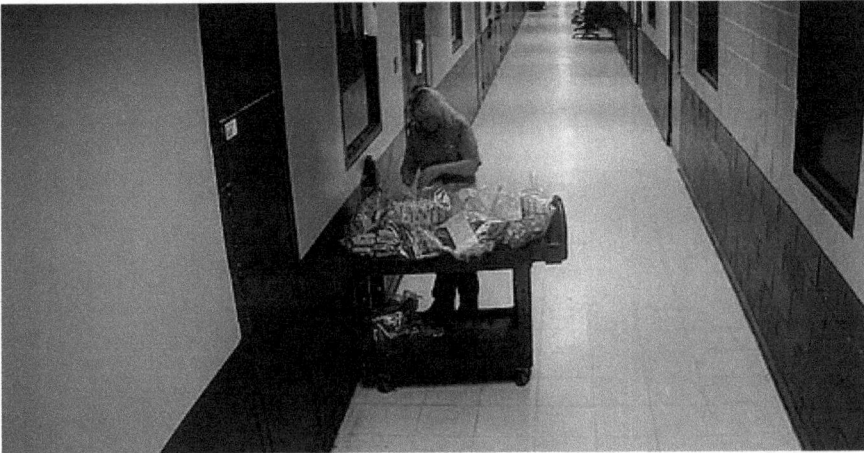

Clip from a video of Vicky passing out commissary orders to inmates. This is actually Casey's cell block, and in the video, you can see him stick his hand out of the serving window and hand Vicky a note. (Lauderdale County Sheriff's Office)

through the notes as, according to inmates, the notes would be destroyed immediately. Maybe it was a simple "I love you" or, perhaps, specific plans on the escape. What we do know is that they obviously, either through the notes, the 959 phone calls while he was at Donaldson Prison, or in personal conversations, had ample opportunities to discuss the planned escape. He was in the LCDC for 63 days between February 25th and June 29th. In fact, again, through our investigation, we learned that Vicky had taken him out of the DC once prior to the escape.

On Wednesday, April 27th, Vicky carried Casey White out of the detention center again under false pretenses. This time they were gone for 9 minutes and 35 seconds according to the security camera footage we found. The footage also revealed that they left through the booking room; however, when they returned less than ten minutes later, a sheriff's patrol car was in the sally port. They reentered the jail through the service door, thus bypassing booking and avoiding being seen by the deputies on site. While we don't know exactly what the purpose of that excursion was, it stands to reason that one thing they certainly discussed was the plans for that Friday.

(Photo by Dan Busey/Times Daily)

CHAPTER 8

The Plan

The escape of Casey White was not a spontaneous decision made on the spur of the moment. It was planned and orchestrated over a period of weeks, if not months. Vicky White used her knowledge of the system, as well as her position as Assistant Director of Corrections, to help Casey White escape.

Once Casey and Vicky made the decision to work together to get him out of jail and prison, several events took place leading up to April 29th. Vicky put her house up for auction on February 10th. It sold later that month, and the sale was finalized just days before the escape. She received a little more than $65,000 dollars on the sale. She also sold one of her vehicles. With no home of her own, she moved in with her parents, where she lived until April the 27th, the last night she spent there.

In the days leading up to April 29th, Vicky had been quietly getting everything ready to execute their plan. Video footage was found at Kohl's Department Store of her shopping in the men's big and tall department and purchasing men's clothes. She was also observed at an adult store where she made purchases. She tried to avoid suspicion by only purchasing one or two items at a time mixed among other items for herself, a tactic she repeated on several occasions.

Shortly after 6:30 p. m. Sunday evening April 24th Vicky showed up at the detention center. She went to her office, where she retrieved information on several individuals who were in the jail's database. One of those individuals was Renee Marie Maxwell, the alias she would use to purchase a vehicle the following day. After about two hours in the office, she left.

Bill of Sale for the Ford Edge Vicky purchased to use as a get-a-way car.
(Lauderdale County Sheriff's Office)

On Monday, April 25th Vicky purchased a 2007 Ford Edge, using the false identity, from a car dealer near Rogersville, Alabama. She paid $5,675 in cash for the vehicle, picked it up the next day, and parked it at the Foodland parking lot at the corner of U. S. Highway 72 and Highway 207 in Rogersville. She was seen on video leaving her personal car at that location and driving the Ford Edge off headed West towards Florence on Wednesday, June 27th. Less than an hour later, she contacted a co-worker, telling her she was stranded at Academy Sports in the Florence Square Shopping Center and needed a ride. The Co-worker picked her up and dropped her off at the Foodland parking lot in Rogersville where she got in her car and drove off. She also rented a room online at the Quality Inn in Florence. The Quality Inn is located just behind Academy Sports. It was in the parking lot of this shopping center where the Ford Edge was parked on Wednesday, and the abandoned patrol car was found on Friday, Vicky reported for work on

Thursday, and it seemed business as usual. She talked with deputies about the transports that were being lined up for the following morning and mentioned that a "murder suspect" was scheduled to appear in court as well. Later that day she turned in retirement papers to Assistant Director Missy Smith. Even though she had been talking about retiring for several months, the quick notice caught everyone by surprise. Her retirement was to be effective the next day.

Foodland Shopping Center in Rogersville, Alabama, where Vicky parked the Ford Edge after purchasing it from a local car dealer. (Photo by Rick Singleton)

The Quality Inn Florence, Alabama
(Photo by Rick Singleton)

When Vicky got off work on Thursday, she pretty much followed her daily routine. She went to her parents' house and had dinner with them. After dinner, she took her dog for a ride. It was at this time things started deviating from her normal routine. She packed some clothes in a gym bag, loaded the bag in her patrol car, and left. This was the last time her parents saw her. She did return a couple of hours later, leaving some personal items in the room she was sleeping in, but those weren't discovered until the next day. Those Items included a will and an insurance policy. She checked into the Comfort in that night. I know a lot of people have speculated, especially on social media, why she would spend her last night in a hotel rather than at home with her parents. I don't know if we'll ever have the answer to that question, but my opinion is Vicky didn't want to face her family that Friday morning. They were a close family, and Vicky loved her dog. I think it would have been too much for her to see them that morning knowing what she was about to do.

Map of Florence Square Shopping Center showing the proximity of Academy
Sports, Quality Inn, and the staging area for the get-a-way car.
(Rick Singleton)

Vicky White leads Casey White out the door of the Lauderdale County
Detention Center beginning an eleven-day national manhunt for the pair.
(Lauderdale County Sheriff's Office) *Note: Time stamp was 10 minutes off. It
was actually 9:40:31 a.m. when they left*

CHAPTER 9

Friday April 29th

April the 29th didn't start out as a typical day at the Lauderdale County Sheriff's Office and it certainly didn't end that way. It was Friday and there was a lot going on. Lieutenant Joe Hamilton was out of the office on the campaign trail. He was running for sheriff as I had announced back in the Fall that I would not be seeking a third term. Chief Deputy Richard Richey and I left shortly after 8:00 a. m. headed to Birmingham, Alabama to attend the academy graduation for our newest deputy. All was good on the home front. Vicky checked out of the hotel and reported to work as usual.

It was a busy day at the detention center. Fridays are hit-and-miss depending on the court dockets. Today was one of those "hits." Assistant Director Vicky White had been talking about retirement for the past few months, and the day before, she filled out her retirement papers. The 29th was to be her last day at work. The sudden announcement

Inmates being escorted to Court.
(Dan Busey/Times Daily)

caught her co-workers off guard so one of them rushed to Walmart to buy her a retirement cake and flowers. They threw together a quick retirement reception as a send-off but later reported that Vicky seemed "out of place." They assumed it was because this was to be her last day at work. She told them she wasn't feeling well, cut the cake, and left the breakroom without eating.

The district court had requested a dozen inmates be brought before the judge for various hearings that morning, so there was a lot of hustle and bustle going on around the DC, especially in the booking area. Two van loads of inmates, one transporting five inmates and the other seven, each with two transport deputies, departed for the courthouse just before 9:00 a.m. leaving a skeleton crew at the detention center. With a staff of forty-two corrections deputies, we had eleven openings on June 29th.

Map of downtown Florence showing proximity of Detention Center to courthouse
(By Rick Singleton)

The short ride to the courthouse, which is just five blocks away, only takes a few minutes. Not long after the second van left Assistant Director White instructed one of the newer corrections deputies to prepare inmate Casey White for transport. This meant that he was to be taken to the booking area, handcuffed, and leg shackles applied with a "rabbit" chain and/or waist chain attached. The deputy complied and placed inmate White on a bench on the far side of the booking room. The booking room had been remodeled a few months earlier to make room for a body scanner that was installed, and, as a result, the area where Casey White was placed was not in view of any security camera. Shortly afterwards, AD Vicky White came into the booking room and told the booking officer that she had an inmate that needed to go to the courthouse for a court-ordered appointment and that since all the armed transport officers were already at the courthouse, she was going to drop him off and turn him over to them. She went on to say that, after she dropped him off, she was going to Med Plus to get checked out because she didn't feel well. She then backed her car into the sally port, entered the booking area, led Casey White out to the waiting patrol car, and drove away.

At 10:18 a.m. Director of Corrections, Jason Butler, texted Vicky asking her to "come up front", meaning the administrative offices. He needed to inform her that she needed to go to the personnel office to complete her paperwork concerning her retirement. When she didn't respond he texted her again at 10:48 a.m. stating that he "assumed" she was still in court but that he needed to see her before she left for the day. Apparently, he learned that she had supposedly gone to Med Plus so at 11:59 a.m., he texted her once again, stating "Just found out you left sick. Hope you feel better." By now, all inmates who had been transported to court that morning had been returned to the detention center, and deputies were handing out lunch trays. At this time, they noticed inmate Casey White had not been returned to the DC and this was reported to the shift sergeant. The sergeant began inquiring if anyone knew why Casey White had not returned with the other inmates. One of the officers she checked with was the booking sergeant who, at that time, wasn't aware he had not returned. The Booking Sergeant immediately began making phone calls to the courthouse and other corrections deputies who were working that morning to see if they knew where inmate White was. At the same time, she began trying to call Vicky White, but her calls went straight to voicemail. As time went on, she became increasingly concerned, and at approximately 3:30 p.m. she notified Assistant Director Missy Smith of the situation. AD Smith in turn notified Lt. Matt Horton of the missing deputy and inmate.

Director of Corrections Jason Butler. (Photo by Dan Busey/Times Daily)

Deputy Sheriff Luke Hinkle celebrates his academy graduation with his parents
on April 29th, 2022.
(Courtesy of Luke Hinkle)

The two-hour drive to Birmingham was uneventful. The chief and I talked about different things, our new deputy, staffing, the upcoming sheriff's race, and more. When we arrived at the academy, we met the new deputy's family. His parents had driven down from Missouri to attend the ceremony. They had made the same trip just a week earlier to attend the academy graduation for his brother, who had recently been employed by the Florence Police Department. There were other family members in attendance, as well as family members of the other graduating officers. When the program was over Chief Richey and I began to make our way home, stopping at one of our favorite lunch spots on that route near Danville, The Old Cook Stove. We arrived back at the office at approximately 3:00 p.m., and I went upstairs to check in. Being Friday afternoon, there weren't many deputies around, so I checked my voice messages, emails, and desk to see if there was anything I needed to tend to before the weekend. On my way out, I stopped by the investigations offices and sat down to talk with Deputy Brandon Graves. While we were talking, he got a phone call from Lieutenant Matt Horton. I noticed he perked up in his chair, and when he hung up the phone, I asked, "What's going on?" He told me Vicky White was missing, and so was Casey White, that she had brought him to the courthouse for a court appearance that morning. He went on to say they hadn't been able to get her on her cell phone and that Casey White had not been returned to the Detention Center with the other inmates. No one knows the gut-wrenching feeling I had in my stomach when I heard those words. My first thought was that Vicky was in extreme danger at best and possibly already dead at worst.

The two of us began a search of the courthouse to determine if the inmate was still there. It was now approximately 3:35 p.m. as we went floor by floor looking for him. During the process Investigator Graves found out that Casey had not been scheduled to be at the courthouse that morning for any reason. On my instructions, other personnel had begun reviewing security footage from the in-house camera system to determine if they made it to the courthouse or not. At the same time, I instructed the staff at the detention center to do the same on their security camera system. I also had our dispatch center contacted to put out a be-on-the-lookout (BOLO) for them and for Vicky's patrol car.

First photos released of Vicky White and Casey white when they were first discovered missing on April 29th. (Lauderdale County Sheriff's Office)

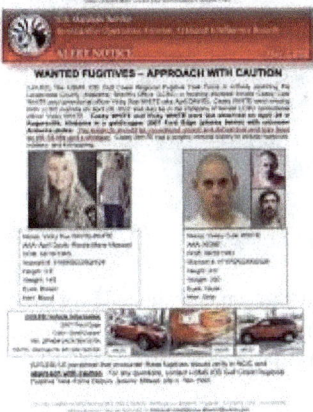

First Wanted Poster distributed by the U. S. Marshals Fugitive Task Force with photos of Ford Edge.
(U. S. Marshals Service)

It wasn't long until we determined that the patrol car never made it to the courthouse. My immediate thought was that Casey White had somehow managed to overpower Vicky and commandeer the vehicle. Realizing by now that they had a six-hour jump on us, I had dispatch send out a national BOLO. I also told them to contact Deputy Quinton Woods and have him notify the United States Marshalls Fugitive Task Force. Deputy Woods had served on that task force for years, even before I took office in 2015. In the meantime, we downloaded the most recent photo we had of the two, along with a photo of the patrol car, and pushed them out to law enforcement across the country.

We got our first tip within the first hour of putting the information out to our deputies and local law enforcement. An employee of the county told us she had seen a patrol car parked in the parking lot of Florence Square Shopping Center when she went for lunch earlier in the day. Deputies were dispatched and found Vicky White's patrol vehicle parked among other vehicles that were advertised for sale. Investigators and deputies descended on the shopping center, canvasing businesses in the area to see if we could identify an escape vehicle as they obviously switched cars at that location.

Photo of Vicky White's patrol vehicle sitting in the parking lot of Florence Square Shopping Center. The photo was taken by a Florence Police Officer at approximately 10:30 a.m. June 29th, less than an hour after Vicky and Casey left the LCDC. (Lauderdale County SO)

When news spread that Vicky's patrol car had been located and where, another sheriff's office employee, Assistant Director of Administration at the Detention Center Missy Smith, contacted us with information that the previous Wednesday she had received a call from Vicky and that she was asking for a ride. Vicky told her she had locked her keys in her car, which was in Rogersville, and that she needed to go home to get the spare key. When she picked Vicky up at Florence Square Shopping Center, in front of Academy Sports, Vicky told her she had found her keys in her purse but had already caught a ride into Florence and couldn't ask the person giving her a ride to turn around and take her back. Missy drove her to Rogersville, Alabama, a small community in the East end of the county. She dropped her off at the Foodland Shopping Center where she got in her personal car and left.

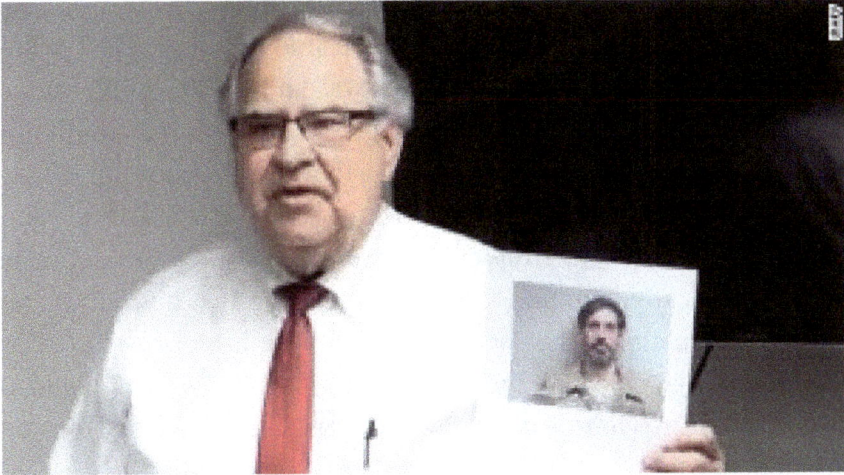

Sheriff Singleton holds up a mug shot of Casey White during the first press conference on Friday night, April 29, 2022. (Photo by Dan Busey/Times Daily)

Later that evening, I called a press conference with our local media to push out the information about the escape and to get Casey and Vicky's photos out to the public. While my initial reaction was that Casey had somehow overpowered Vicky and took her against her will, the first pieces of the puzzle had already started falling into place. There was no scheduled appointment at the courthouse, so Vicky obviously lied about that to her co-workers. The video footage from the detention center made it clear that Vicky led Casey White out the door, against protocol and in violation of departmental policy. This was not the Vicky White we knew and had worked with for the past sixteen

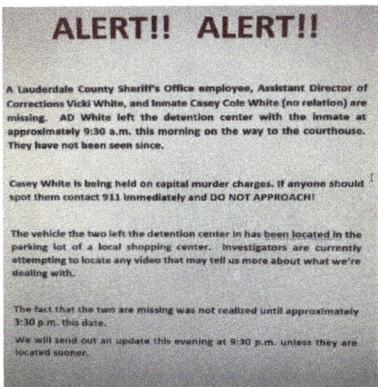

ALERT!! ALERT!!

A Lauderdale County Sheriff's Office employee, Assistant Director of Corrections Vicki White, and Inmate Casey Cole White (no relation) are missing. AD White left the detention center with the inmate at approximately 9:30 a.m. this morning on the way to the courthouse. They have not been seen since.

Casey White is being held on capital murder charges. If anyone should spot them contact 911 immediately and DO NOT APPROACH!

The vehicle the two left the detention center in has been located in the parking lot of a local shopping center. Investigators are currently attempting to locate any video that may tell us more about what we're dealing with.

The fact that the two are missing was not realized until approximately 3:30 p.m. this date.

We will send out an update this evening at 9:30 p.m. unless they are located sooner.

Alert sent to local law enforcement and news outlets within minutes of discovering Casey and Vicky White were missing. (Lauderdale County Sheriff's Office)

years, but it was apparent that she had not been forced against her will. That could only mean she willingly participated and, if that was the case, there was only one explanation for those of us that knew her; she had been threatened or coerced into helping Casey White escape. In either case, we knew she was in danger. As the hours dragged on, Deputy US Marshalls began to arrive at the courthouse and set up a "war" room from which they would coordinate their efforts in locating the pair for the next several days. It was close to midnight by now, and I reluctantly went home to try to get some rest. As you can imagine, I got very little sleep that night. Day one had come to a close, and we had no idea what kind of vehicle they were in or what direction they were headed. By now, they could be anywhere from Detroit, Chicago, Kansas City, Dallas, Houston, Orlando, Washington D.C., or anywhere in between.

Local media attend a press conference at the Lauderdale County Courthouse.
(Photo by Rick Singleton)

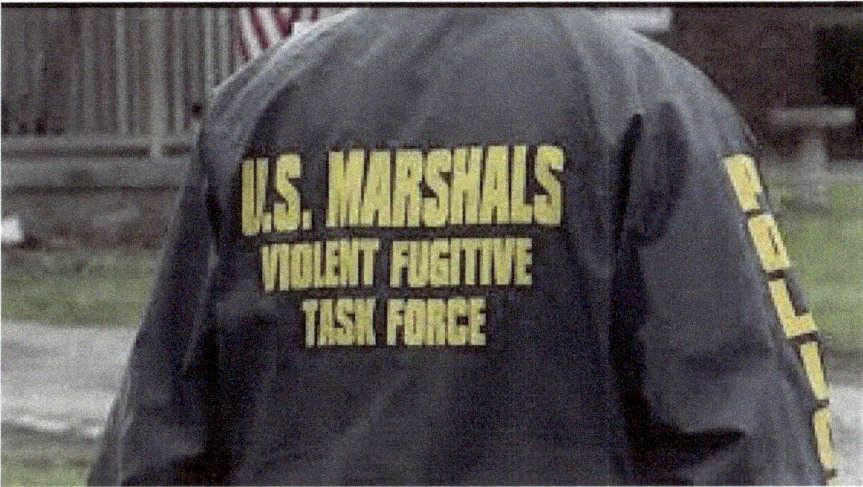

(United States Marshalls Service)

CHAPTER 10

On The Run: A National Manhunt Begins

The first Deputy United States Marshalls arrived at the sheriff's office late Friday night. Working with our deputies and investigators, they immediately began reviewing what we knew at that point. What we did know was they left the detention center together at 9:41 a. m. and Vicky's patrol car had been found parked in the Florence Square Shopping Center parking lot. We knew it had been there since about 10:30 a. m. and that the handcuffs, leg shackles, rabbit chain, a handcuff key, and some of her department equipment were in the car. Later that evening, we discovered that she had spent the night at the Quality Inn. We were unsuccessful in finding any surveillance video footage of any vehicle they may have switched to when they abandoned the patrol car.

Times Daily headlines concerning
U. S. Marshals joining search.
(Courtesy of Times Daily)

While some of the investigators worked well into the early morning hours, more fugitive task force deputies arrived on Saturday. The "war room" was set up in the conference room in the sheriff's office. Investigators picked up their canvas of the area around the shopping center, expanding their search for any possible leads from surveillance cameras in the area. In the meantime, we got the footage of Vicky and Casey leaving the detention center and pushed it out to the media. We were also able to get a more current photo of Casey White. Casey was known for changing his appearance and it had changed considerably since he was booked into the DC in February.

Based on the information from AD Smith, investigators went to Rogersville to see if they could find anything on video around the

Casey White on the morning of April 29th as he is led from his cell to the booking room to be prepared for transport. (Lauderdale County Sheriff's Office)

Foodland shopping center. They were able to identify Vicky and, although it was very blurry due to the distance, saw her around a red or orange colored vehicle in the parking lot. This was the first actual lead that developed as to what vehicle they may have left the area in, but the video was so bad that all we could gather was it was a small SUV orange or red in color.

Map showing proximity of where Ford Edge was abandoned on 4/29 and phone pinged on 4/30. (By Rick Singleton)

Later that evening marshals got a "ping" from one of the phones Vicky had purchased in preparation for the escape. They had discovered the phone number while searching a storage unit Vicky had rented. The phone was immediately turned off again, but we had a possible location. The phone "pinged" in a rural area just north of Springhill, Tennessee. Deputies left immediately and headed to the area. Chief

Marie Waxwel, local reporter with WAAY 31 News in Huntsville, interviews Sheriff Singleton outside the Lauderdale County Detention Center while Vicky and Casey were on the run. (WAAY 31 News)

Deputy Richard Richey and I joined them a little later. I certainly wanted to be there when they were found, and obviously, I was hoping that would be the case. The investigators spent several hours scouring the area but didn't turn up any leads. After a couple of hours, Chief Richey and I headed back to Alabama. Discussing the case and the fact that we had very little to go on at that point, I commented to the chief that if we didn't get them back in custody within a couple of days, I felt the national media would pick up on it. The next night, I had my first contact with a national news outlet, and by Monday morning, crews from CNN, FOX, NBC News, News Nation, and others began arriving in town. The first major break came on Sunday night, May 1st. A man called in a tip in response to a news report that the patrol car had been abandoned in the shopping center parking lot, among other vehicles that were for sale. He stated he had been looking at the cars parked there Thursday night and seen an orange Ford Edge that he was interested in. He was looking at the cars and the Edge stood out because, when he

Ford Edge used in escape. Notice what the witness described as what looked like a "bullet hole" in the lower left bumper. (Lauderdale County Sheriff's Office)

went to look, there was no for sale sign or phone number on the vehicle. He also noticed there was no license plate and described the vehicle as having minor damage and what looked like a "bullet hole" in the rear bumper. When he looked inside, he noticed several items including a duffle bag. The vehicle matched the description of the one Vicky White was seen getting into at the Rogersville Foodland parking lot the previous day. When investigators canvassed the area Friday afternoon, the Ford Edge was gone.

The vehicle description was confirmed late Sunday evening when the seller of the vehicle was identified and confirmed that he sold the vehicle to a lady by the name of Renee Marie Maxwell, one of the names obtained by Vicky from the detention center database. A national BOLO was issued with the vehicle description "for law enforcement only" but mid-day Monday, inadvertently and under the pretense of helping get the word out, a local law enforcement agency posted the vehicle description on their social media page. By the time it was discovered, the post had already been shared more than 170 times. The information had been disseminated as "law enforcement only" to give law enforcement an opportunity to locate it before Vicky and Casey found out we had identified the vehicle they left in. We knew they would ditch the vehicle as soon as word got out that we had it identified. At the time, I saw the leak as a major setback. Investigators had worked around the clock all weekend to finally get a break, and now they would know we were onto them. As it turned out, it was really a blessing in disguise.

A press conference was called Monday afternoon, May 2nd, to put the vehicle description out to the public. That morning, I was informed that a warrant had been obtained by the investigators for Vicky White. The charge was "Aiding and/or Facilitating an Escape" in the first degree. They determined early on that she was a willing participant in the escape. In fact, the warrant was obtained later Friday night, April 29th, the same day they left the detention center. However, they withheld that information from me at first because I was still reluctant to accept the fact that she was not somehow coerced or threatened to get her assistance. The information from the press conference was shared around the world by national and international media outlets. This was the second press conference held regarding the escape, and it was attended by local and national media. We soon begin receiving tips of the vehicle being spotted from as far away as Washington state.

Sheriff Rick Singleton addresses the local and national news media at a press conference on Monday, May 2nd. Announcing a warrant had been issued for Vicky White. (Photo WAAY Channel 31)

United States Marshall for the Northern District of Alabama, Marty Keely, addresses the media regarding the vehicle identified as the get-a-way car the White's left Florence in.
(Photo by Dan Busey/Times Daily)

State of Alabama Unified Judicial System Form CR-58 Rev. 8/98	**WARRANT OF ARREST** (Felonies, Misdemeanors, or Violations)	**Warrant Number** 41-WR-2022-900529.00 **Case Number** DA 22-481

IN THE DISTRICT COURT OF LAUDERDALE COUNTY, ALABAMA

STATE OF ALABAMA v. VICKY SUE DAVIS WHITE

TO ANY LAW ENFORCEMENT OFFICER WITHIN THE STATE OF ALABAMA:

☑ Probable cause has been found on a Complaint filed in the court against (name or description of person to be arrested)

VICKY SUE DAVIS WHITE

charging the offense of

1. PERMITING/AIDING ESCAPE 1 - 13A-010-034

as described in the Complaint.

☐ An Indictment has been returned by the grand jury of this county against (name or description of person to be arrested)

charging the offense of

☑ YOU ARE THEREFORE ORDERED to arrest the person named or described above and bring that person before a judge or magistrate of this court to answer the charges against that person and have with you then and have this Warrant of Arrest with your return thereon. If a judge or magistrate of this court is unavailable. or if the arrest is made in another county. you shall take the accused person before the nearest or most accessible judge or magistrate in the county of arrest.

☐ You may release the accused person without taking the accused person before a judge or magistrate:
    ☐ If the accused person enters into a bond in the amount of $ _____ with cash or sufficient sureties by an approved professional bonding company or property with the court clerk.
    ☐ If the accused person posts a cash bond in the amount of $ _____ with the court clerk.
    ☐ On his or her personal recognizance
    Bond Conditions:

☐ No Bond

DONE this 29th day of April, 2022

_____   /s/AUDRA WALLACE
Date   Judge/Court Clerk/Magistrate/Warrant Clerk

Copy of arrest warrant issued for Vicky White by the court.
(Lauderdale County Sheriff's Office)

CHAPTER 11

Looking For a Needle In A Haystack:

The First Seven Days:

When Vicky and Casey left the Lauderdale County Detention Center on April 29th, they had a six-hour head start. By that afternoon, when we realized they were gone, they could have been several states away. They knew everything, where they were headed, what they were driving, and we knew nothing other than they were gone. It was literally like looking for a needle in a haystack.

Sheriff Rick Singleton appears on a National News Broadcast discussing the escape and encouraging citizens if they "see something, say something". He constantly stressed that it would be a tip from the public that would lead to the capture of Vicky and Casey White. (Photo by al.com)

By Monday, we had finally been able to identify the vehicle they left the Florence area in, but due to the leak we knew they would ditch it at their first opportunity, putting us back to square one as to what kind of vehicle we needed to be looking for. We also knew the Ford Edge would turn up now, the question was when and where. As the hours passed, I realized we would at least know what direction they left in when we did find the vehicle, and that was more than we knew at this point. It was sort of the silver lining in the cloud.

Over the next few days tips came in from all over the country. They were spotted at a gas station in Washington state. Vicky had walked into a convenience store in Florida and given the clerk a note stating: "I am Vicky White. I've been kidnapped. Help me." Other reports came in that they were seen in Tennessee, Kentucky, and even in Lauderdale County. One promising lead was from Ohio that a tall man was looking into the windows of a home, and when he was spotted, he ran, jumped into an orange SUV that was being driven by a woman, and left at a high rate of speed. None of these leads panned out, and there were dozens of them. Hundreds of tips were received from all points of the continental U. S. The last lead that came into the sheriff's office was received at 12:56 p.m. on May 9th, just hours before they were captured. It was from a local television station that had received a call that the pair were seen in Arkansas in a U-Haul truck. I received this information personally on my office phone. By then, we knew they had been in Evansville, so it was very possible they had left and were headed west. I saw the information as a potentially credible lead at the time.

Vicky Whites former home in Lexington, Alabama. (WAAY TV)

Other than identifying the escape vehicle, no major leads were developed the first seven days in terms of their direction or mode of travel. Locally, investigators continued following up on information about Vicky's actions leading up to April 29th. She had sold her home by means of an online auction and collected approximately $65,000 from the sale just a few days before the escape. She had also sold one of the two vehicles she owned. In addition, she was on video shopping at a local department store in the men's big and tall section as well as at an adult store. And, of course, she had purchased the Ford Edge under an alias and paid cash.

Vicky White's mother gave an exclusive interview to WAAY 31, a Huntsville television statement, about her daughter and the last time she saw/spoke to her. She asked that her face not be shown during the interview. (Used with permission of WAAY TV)

Her parents, who were very cooperative and helpful even though extremely distraught, shared with investigators Vicky's activities and actions the night before they left. According to them, she came in after work and had supper with them as she normally did. After supper, she took her dog on a ride and then returned to their home, where she had been staying since she sold her house. Shortly after, she left, and they never saw or spoke to her again. She did return a couple of hours later and placed some personal belongings on her bed, but her parents weren't aware and the items weren't discovered until later the next day. She had never mentioned Casey White to them nor what she was planning. They, like her friends and co-workers, were caught totally off-guard and could not believe that she would do such a thing.

Bordering the states of Tennessee and Mississippi, and her sharing with co-workers that she wanted to move to the beach, we were certain they had left the area and more than likely left the state. The decision in the first couple of hours after the escape to request the assistance of the USMFTF was a no-brainer. The technology, manpower, and other resources they had at their disposal would be needed. We knew we didn't have the resources to look for them on our own when they could be anywhere in the country, or out of the country for that matter. It had been a week since they left, and we still had no clue what direction they went or what they were driving.

Vicky's bedroom at her parent's house as investigators found it on the afternoon of April 29th. (Lauderdale County Sheriff's Office)
Sheriff Rik Singleton and District Attorney Chris Conolly address the media at a press conference on Friday, May 9th, announcing that the Ford Edge had been located in Springhill Tennessee where it was abandoned within hours of the escape on April 29th. (Photo by Dan Busey/Times Daily)

Sheriff Rik Singleton and District Attorney Chris Conolly address the media at a press conference on Friday, May 9th, announcing that the Ford Edge had been located in Springhill Tennessee where it was abandoned within hours of the escape on April 29th. (Photo by Dan Busey/Times Daily)

The Ford Edge had not turned up anywhere and then, on Friday, May 6th, we got the call we had been waiting on. A wrecker driver near Springhill, Tennessee saw the description of the get-a-way car on the news and remembered towing a similar vehicle the Friday before. He went to check and, sure enough, it matched the description. He called the local sheriff's office, and they in turn, contacted the Marshall's service. Finally, we had a break in the case. The investigators immediately sprang into action, traveling to Tennessee to process the vehicle and canvass the area to see what additional information they could develop as to the whereabouts of Vicky and Casey White. The first order of business was to determine if any vehicles had been reported stolen in the area around the time the Edge was abandoned.

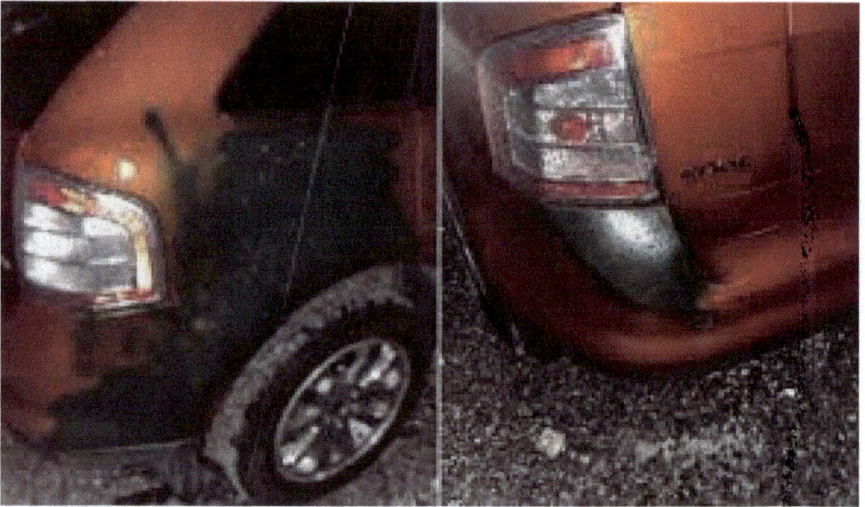

A botched paint job in an attempt to disguise the get-a-way vehicle.
(Lauderdale County Sheriff's Office)

We called our third press conference to release this information to the media, who had been giving wide coverage to the search, not only for Casey and Vicky, but for the Ford Edge as well. It was held in the Probate Judges courtroom inside the courthouse.

CHAPTER 12

Hot Pursuit: May 6th

Having left Florence at approximately 10:00 a.m. on the morning of April 29th, the Ford Edge had been abandoned less than four hours later just east of Springhill, Tennessee, about two hours north of Florence. At first, since it was abandoned so soon, we felt like the SUV had experienced mechanical problems because of when, where, and how it had been abandoned. We didn't really think it was planned, and apparently it wasn't. As the pair headed north, they stopped at a Dollar General store and bought several cans of green spray paint. They had apparently intended to disguise the vehicle by painting it green. Investigators later learned that Casey was upset about the vehicle being bright orange and, after the attempt to paint it was unsuccessful, ultimately decided to dump it. They left the SUV on the side of the road after purchasing a pick-up truck that was sitting in a yard for sale.

A local resident saw the abandoned Ford Edge and called the Williamson County Sheriff's Office at approximately 1:30 p.m., just three and one-half hours after the pair left Florence. She felt it posed a traffic hazard because it was left at an intersection, and she was concerned the school bus, which was scheduled to run in just a couple of hours, would not be able to make the turn with the vehicle sitting there. Leaving the vehicle there was a major mistake on their part. On the side of the road and blocking an intersection, it was going to come to the attention of law enforcement. Had they left it in a major parking lot in nearby Springhill Tennessee it may have taken much longer for law enforcement to track it down.

The Ford Edge parked in the impound lot near Springhill, Tennessee
(Lauderdale County Sheriff's Office)

When the deputy ran the VIN number the vehicle came back "not stolen" because it had been purchased by Vicky, and with no license plate, there was no way to determine who the SUV belonged to. The deputy had the vehicle towed, and it had been sitting in the wrecker lot for a week. The SUV had been abandoned and towed before we even knew Casey White had escaped with Vicky's help. The only thing left in the Ford Edge were several cans of spray paint. It was determined they had been purchased at a Dollar General in Mt. Pleasant, Tennessee.

While talking with residents in the immediate area of where the Ford Edge was abandoned, investigators found a home with vehicles sitting in the yard for sale. When they spoke with the resident, he stated he had sold a truck to a tall man the previous Friday, and when he drove the truck off, an orange Ford Edge driven by a female followed him. The truck did not have a license plate, but the man who bought the truck wanted one, so he put a plate on it for him. He didn't have the plate number, but he did have the VIN number.

The pickup truck purchased by Casey White near Springhill, Tennessee. (United States Marshalls Service)

Armed with that information, the marshals began searching databases and license plate scanners in an attempt to locate the truck. The location of the Ford Edge and identifying the vehicle they left that area in was critical in the search to find Casey and Vicky White. After getting that information, it was less than 72 hours when Vicky and Casey White would be located and taken into custody.

Mr. James Stinson, owner of the carwash where Casey and Vicky abandoned the truck they bought in Tennessee. (WEVV TV)

CHAPTER 13

The Road to Evansville: May 9th

Equipped with the VIN number and description of the pickup truck, investigators began using the resources available to them to locate the truck. The VIN was entered in the National Crime Information Centers data base, and it was just a matter of time until they would be able to locate it. Within a few hours, they struck paydirt. An officer with the Evansville, Indiana police department had taken a report of an abandoned vehicle at a local carwash. The owner of the carwash, James Stinson, had called about a truck left at the carwash that had been there a couple of days. What struck him as odd was that the window was down, and the keys were in the vehicle. Apparently, Casey was counting on someone stealing the truck off the carwash lot. That was on Wednesday, May 4th. The officer ran the VIN to determine if the vehicle was stolen. When it came back clean, he informed Mr. Stinson that since the vehicle wasn't stolen and on private property, there was nothing he could do. Mr. Stinson then had the truck towed off his lot.

James Stinson's carwash in Evansville, Indiana. Had he not reported the abandoned truck to law enforcement it could have taken much longer to find it, and the Whites. (WEVV TV)

It was late Sunday night, May 8th when the marshals got the "hit" they were waiting for from NCIC. They called me at home and told me the truck had been checked through NCIC in Evansville Indiana and that they were leaving immediately heading up there. Agents with the local Great Lakes Regional Fugitive Task Force were also alerted and converged on the city. Monday morning, they went to the carwash to review video footage and positively identified Casey White on the video with the truck. They also saw him get into a gray Cadillac driven by a female and leave the area. The search was now focused on finding the Cadillac. Investigators and local law enforcement officers began canvassing the area. An off-duty investigator with the Evansville Police Department found the vehicle parked at Motel 41 that afternoon. Agents immediately set up surveillance and were in the process of developing a plan of action when they saw Vicky White exit room 150 wearing a wig. Casey came out afterwards, on crutches, and they both got into the Cadillac with Casey behind the wheel. Agents fell in behind them, but it wasn't long until they were spotted by Casey and Vicky.

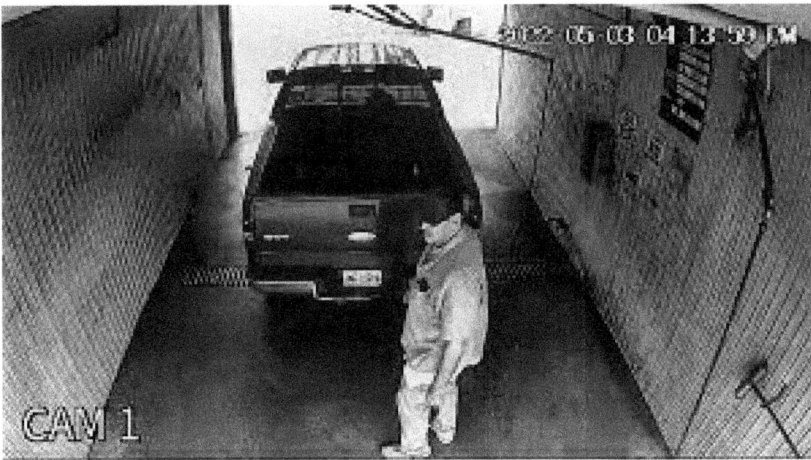

Casey White seen on video at the carwash.
(Courtesy of James Stinson)

El'Agance Shemwell, a reporter for WEVV news, interviews James Stinson about the Casey White case on Monday, May 9th, 2022. Mr. Stinson reported the abandoned truck to Evansville Police the previous week. (With permission of WEVV TV)

Vicky and Casey had rented this motel room for 14 days. The gray Cadillac was spotted in the parking lot and shortly after Vicky and Casey were seen leaving the room. Within a matter of minutes Casey was in custody and Vicky was on her way to the hospital with a bullet wound to the head. (Lauderdale County Sheriff's Office)

They attempted to run from the officers, and a pursuit ensued, ending with marshals ramming the Cadillac. Casey White immediately attempted to leave the vehicle from the driver's side door but saw another police vehicle headed directly for him. He retreated into the vehicle just before it was rammed and pushed into the ditch. He then exited with his hands raised and told the agents,"Help my wife. She just shot herself. I didn't do it." Officers took him into custody while other officers and agents went to arrest Vicky. One officer was heard over the police radio saying, "she still has the gun in her hand and her finger on the trigger."

Marshals rammed the Cadillac, pushing it into a ditch. The hunt for Vicky and Casey White was over.
(Vandenburg County Sheriff's Office, Indiana)

Vicky White lies on the ground outside the wrecked Cadillac while officers render first aid. She was transported to the hospital where she died the next day.
(Vanderburg County Sheriff's Office)

Casey White taken into custody by Vandenburg County officers after 11 days on the run.
(Vandenburg County Sheriff's Office, Indiana)

Working cautiously, they were able to secure the weapon and get Vicky out of the car. She was transported to the local hospital but, according to officers on the scene, it didn't "look good".

With the two now in custody and under control, marshals and investigators with the Vandenburg County Sheriff's Office began collecting evidence. Among the items recovered was close to $30,000 in cash, several weapons, a wig, and camping equipment. Casey would later tell Sheriff Wedding of Vandenburg County that he had planned to engage the officers in a shootout but lost control of his weapon during the crash. This was an outcome that those of us who knew Casey thought might play out when he was cornered. Luckily, he didn't get the chance.

Word began to spread, not only throughout the Evansville area, but to the media as well. Some of the national media teams had gone to Evansville earlier that day and were on the scene within minutes of the crash. We called our fourth and final press conference in front of the Lauderdale County Courthouse and put out the news that Casey was in custody and Vicky was in the hospital with a gunshot wound to the head. Questions about who actually fired the shot that struck Vicky were asked immediately. At the time it was still unclear who fired the shot, officers at the scene, Casey White, or Vicky. As more information came in it was evident that Vicky fired the shot as the gun was still clutched tightly in her right hand when it was removed by the officer on the scene. Later that evening Sheriff Wedding of Vandenburg County also called a press conference where he released details of the chase and the evidence collected at the scene.

Evidence collected from the Whites' vehicle after they were captured in Evansville Indiana.
(Vandenburg County Sheriff's Office, Indiana)

Sheriff Rick Singleton holds a press conference announcing the capture of Casey and Vicky White in Evansville, Indiana. He is accompanied by Sgt. Shane Keeton who had served as the sheriff's point-of-contact with the media throughout the nation-wide manhunt. (Used with permission of WHNT TV, Huntsville, Alabama)

Sheriff Dave Wedding of Vandenburg County Indiana holds a press conference after the capture of Casey and Vicky White in Evansville, Indiana. (WEVV TV)

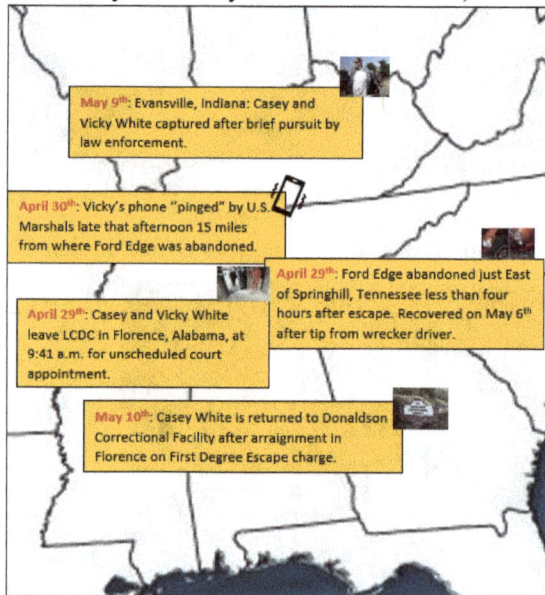

Map showing timeline and location of major events in the search for Vicky and Casey White.
(By Rick Singleton)

Casey White is escorted into the Lauderdale County Courthouse by members of
the transport team.
(Photo by Dan Busey/Times Daily)

Below: Transcription of letters written by Casey White while on the run. The letters were found in the Cadillac when it was searched for evidence. (Lauderdale County Sheriff's Office)

Well, it's crazy, it's a long story, and I don't have time just to make sure everyone gets their letter. I hope I've not caused you much trouble with all this. I am so happy my wife loves me so much. It was the best when I got out. I wish I could see y'all.

When we get caught, she wants me where to shoot her. I hate to. I don't know if I can, but I've got to. We had plans, so I didn't want you to think I was a killer.

And I love you with all mine.

And I know you love me with all yours.

And don't dwell on this. I was not ever going to get out, And I was sick of doing time. My beautiful wife gave me this chance, and I took it. I will die as a happy man. She treats me so well. I got nice clothes and good food.

Casey Cole White

May 2nd 2022

This is Casey Cole White. And me and my wife are all over the news. Y'all are stupid. Anyway, I don't think we will make it much longer. But you never know. I just wanted y'all to know I never killed anyone. But my beautiful wife wants me to shoot her when and if y'all catch us. Make sure my parents + kids know she wanted me to, so we go together. Tell my family I couldn't take prison no more and thought I might as well for sure if I can get a few sorry S.O.B. of the system.

Casey White

This is Casey Cole White. By now, if you're reading this letter I'am.(dead)

I made Vicky White get me out and send me money to prison.

I've done wrong but done right. (Also) Limestone County give me 75 yrs. for killing a dog, shooting some holes in the sheetrock, and pointing a gun at AL for 2 seconds.

CHAPTER 14

Casey And Vicky Return to Alabama

Investigators with the U. S. Marshals service and the Vanderburgh County Sheriff's Office interviewed Casey White after he was captured on May 9th. According to Sheriff Wedding, Casey stated he had intended to "have a shootout with police if it came to that", but when marshals rammed their vehicle, he lost his weapon. That was certainly a scenario that we were all concerned about given his violent history and the fact that he was facing the death penalty in Alabama for the murder of Connie Ridgeway. Casey had proven numerous times he could be a dangerous individual and, if cornered, certainly had the propensity to be violent. That was the reason, from day one, we emphasized the risk to our law enforcement partners across the country he would pose when confronted. Thankfully, at least in that regard, it ended well. The next morning, Casey waived extradition and could be returned to Alabama. In the early days of the escape, in anticipation and expectation of their eventual capture, the Lauderdale County Sheriff's office had made arrangements as to where the pair would be incarcerated upon their return. A neighboring county had agreed to house Vicky White. For obvious reasons we could not house her in our own facility. As for Casey, the Alabama Department of Corrections had agreed to allow us to return him to the Donaldson Correctional Facility immediately after his arraignment before the Lauderdale County Circuit Court, regardless of the time of day or night.

Weapons recovered by Indiana law enforcement officers and United States Marshalls when Casey White was taken into custody on May 9th, 2022. Also taken was Vicky White's duty belt she was wearing on the day of the escape. (Vandenburg County Sheriff's Office, Indiana)

Some of the LCSO investigators drove to Evansville Tuesday, May 10th, to meet with Vandenburgh County investigators and to retrieve what evidence had been collected by them during the capture. We also put together a special transport team after their capture in preparation to bring him back to Alabama. The team, comprised of members of the Florence/Lauderdale County Special Operations Team, was ready to go in the event he waived extradition, which he did. They left for Evansville mid-morning on the 10th and returned to the courthouse at approximately 10:30 p.m. that night with Casey in tow. He immediately appeared before Judge Ben Graves for his initial advisement of the charges against him. His attorneys met with him briefly before the hearing. Several members of the local and national media attended along with members of Connie Ridgeways family. The hearing lasted approximately fifteen minutes and concluded with the Judge ordering him remanded to the custody of the Alabama Department of Corrections immediately. He was escorted back to the transport van and departed for Donaldson Correctional Facility as had been previously arranged.

Casey White is escorted from the Lauderdale County Courthouse after appearing before Judge Ben Graves for his advisement on escape charges. He was transported immediately to the Donaldson Correctional Facility in Bessemer, Alabama where he was serving 75 years for a crime spree in 2015.
(Lauderdale County Sheriff's Office)

In the meantime, Vicky White had been in the Intensive Care Unit at a hospital in Evansville where she was being treated for a gunshot wound to the head. During the crash a single shot was fired, and the evidence was clear it was she who fired the weapon. The gun was clutched tightly in her right hand, and she was sitting on the passenger's side of the vehicle. She eventually succumbed to her wounds and an autopsy was performed by the Vandenburgh County Coroner. The cause of death was listed as "self-inflicted gunshot wound to the head".

(Courtesy of Times Daily)

It was reported that her death was a suicide, but some of us wondered if it could have been accidental. I know Casey stated she "shot herself" and the evidence, as I said, supports that statement, but could the shot have been fired accidentally as a result of the impact from the crash?

In the 911 call during the pursuit, you can hear Vicky talking to Casey. Her tone of voice is one of desperation, but

Funeral service for Corrections Officer Vicky White (Used with permission of WAAY Channel 31, Huntsville, Alabama)

her comments, to me at least, tell me she was desperate to get away. 'The airbags are going to go off and kill us". "Let's get out and run!" "We should have never left the f…ing motel!" What I did not hear was "we can't get caught," "I can't go back to Alabama," "I can't go to prison" or "I love you!" Those are the kind of comments I would expect from someone in that situation who was contemplating suicide. Also, Casey had tried to exit the vehicle before it was rammed a second time and pushed into the ditch. That means he was not buckled in which in turn means he would have been lying on top of Vicky. Officers heard the shot as they approached the vehicle. Casey then stood up with his hands out the driver's side window and was more than likely stepping on Vicky. In the commotion could he have inadvertently caused the gun to go off? I was not there, and I do not know for a fact what happened, but based on statements of the officers who *were* on the scene, the shot was fired after the second ramming and before Casey was pulled from the vehicle. Also, the trajectory of the bullet was not, in my opinion, consistent with suicide. The shot entered from front to back, entering at the right side of the forehead at the hairline and exiting from the rear top portion about the middle of the skull with an upward angle. The bullet also grazed Casey across the back of his neck so it would seem his head had to be close to hers when the shot was fired. If he was already standing up there is no way the bullet could have grazed him across the back of his neck. Taking this into consideration it seems very plausible to me that the shot could very well have been accidental.

Vicky in Happier Times

Regardless, Vicky White did not survive and took the answer to this and several other questions to her grave. She was buried in Lauderdale County on Saturday, May 14th. There were approximately 200 people in attendance, her family, friends, some co-workers, and former inmates of the LCDC. I did not attend, but I did send my condolences via one of my deputies, who was a close friend to the family. I felt my attendance would be a distraction given the media attention and wasn't sure, under the circumstances, if the family would want me there.

Casey White sits at the defendants table in Judge Benn Graves courtroom
accompanied by his attorneys. (WHNT TV)

CHAPTER 15

Casey Faces New Charges, Or Does He?

On June 9th, in a surprise move, District Attorney Chris Connolly filed a motion with the Lauderdale County Circuit Court to "nolle prosequi with leave to reinstate" (not to prosecute) the escape charge against Casey White. The judge granted the order, and the Escape in the First-Degree charge was dropped. The media was abuzz wondering "what's going on?" The move certainly caught everyone off guard. The answer would come three days later on July 12th when the DA announced that Casey White had been indicted on a count of felony murder in the death of Vicky White stating "during the course of and in furtherance of committing Escape in the First Degree, White caused the death of Vicky White, who died from a gunshot wound to the head". The Alabama Criminal Code allows for a person to be charged with felony murder when they are committing other felonies and cause the death of someone. Escape in the First Degree is one of those felonies, and in the case of the murder charge, it is a lesser, included offense.

Also, on July 21st, the Federal Government announced that they were charging Casey White with weapons violations in Indiana. At the time of his capture, Casey had in his possession an AR-15 rifle and four handguns. Vicky had purchased these weapons, some in the days leading up to the escape. As a convicted felon he was in violation by having weapons in his possession.

"Alabama Code Title 13A-6-2:

A person commits the crime of murder if he or she does any of the following:

(3) He or she commits or attempts to commit arson in the first degree, burglary in the first or second degree, escape in the first degree, kidnapping in the first degree, rape in the first degree, robbery in any degree, sodomy in the first degree, aggravated child abuse under Section 26-15-3.1, or any other felony clearly dangerous to human life and, in the course of and in furtherance of the crime that he or she is committing or attempting to commit, or in immediate flight therefrom, he or she, or another participant if there be any, causes the death of any person."

Casey White appears in court in Lauderdale County, Alabama with his team of lawyers for a hearing after his capture. (Used with permission of WAAY Channel 31, Huntsville, Alabama)

With the added charges, Casey White was now facing two separate counts of murder in Alabama as well as charges in the Federal Court system for possession of weapons. On May 4, 2023, there was yet another bizarre twist concerning the charges against Casey White. In a surprise move that caught even his own attorneys off guard, Casey entered a guilty plea to escape in the 1st Degree, the same charge that had been dropped just eleven months earlier. The plea was the result of a plea bargain with the District Attorney, Chris Connoly. In exchange, the murder charge in the death of Vicky White would be dropped, and he would receive a life sentence for the escape. He returned to the court for a sentencing hearing on June 8th and was given the life sentence as agreed to. With the seventy-five-year sentence he was already serving and a life sentence on top of that, he won't be eligible for parole until 2081. Barring another

(Courtesy of Times Daily)

Lauderdale County, Alabama,
District Attorney Chris Connoly
(Courtesy off the Lauderdale County
District Attorney's Office)

escape, he will never leave the walls of Donaldson Prison again. In his statement to the court, Casey said, "I feel like the most hated man in the world." He also apologized to Vicky's family and declared his love for the woman who helped him escape. "She was the first person who cared about me in six years," he said. Was his love genuine? I'm sure there are those who believe him, but for me, *the proof is in the pudding*. To me, he never showed any real emotion after Vicky's death and, in fact, was communicating with other women within a week of his capture and return to Donaldson prison. The one thing I am finally convinced of, though is that Vicky White did indeed love him. She gave up everything she had, including her life, for this man. There's only one reason I know of why someone would do that, true love. In the end, she, like so many others before her, fell victim to manipulation by an inmate. Theres no question in my mind that he used her to get what he wanted, out of jail and prison. Remember, he was planning an escape the first time he was in the Lauderdale County Detention center back in 2020, before he even knew Vicky White. He apparently picked up on her vulnerability then and began making his move. Between 2020 and his second incarceration at LCDC in 2021, they talked on the phone some 80 times. When he came back for this second stay is obviously when he really made his move. After returning to Donaldson in 2021, they talked more than 900 times before his final move back to Lauderdale County in February 2022. That was an average of more than four calls per day.

But the story doesn't end there. On July 28th, 2023, the DA made another surprise announcement. He filed a motion with the court to "Nolle Pross With Leave to Reinstate" the murder charge against Casey concerning the death of Connie Ridgeway. The announcement was made after consultation with Connie's sons, Austin and Cameron Williams.

NEWS RELEASE

Date: July 28, 2023

Capital Murder Charge in the Death of Connie Ridgeway Suspended

The Lauderdale County District Attorney's Office announced today that the Capital Murder charges against Casey White have been suspended, with leave to reinstate in the future. The DA's office filed a "Motion to Nolle Pros with Leave to Reinstate" today. (Copy of Motion attached)

Among the reasons cited for the case being placed on hold is the fact that White is already serving what amounts to a life without parole prison sentence and the amount of State resources which will be required to go forward with a jury trial at this time.

In addition to serving a life sentence for his 2022 escape from the Lauderdale County Detention Center, White is serving a total of 75 years in prison based on convictions in Limestone County in February 2019. According to prison officials, he will not be eligible to even be considered for parole until 2081, at which time he will be 98 years old.

Lauderdale County District Attorney Chris Connolly said the decision to suspend the capital murder case was made after discussions with investigators and with Connie Ridgeway's two adult children Austin and Cameron Williams. Investigators are continuing the investigation into the Connie Ridgeway murder. The investigation is focusing on whether there are others, in addition to Casey White, involved in the 2015 murder.

According to Connolly, "Austin and Cameron support the decision to suspend the prosecution at this time. Suspending the prosecution of Casey White will allow investigators additional time to complete their investigation and will preserve State resources. In the meantime, Casey White is right where he belongs; in Donaldson Prison."

As are all Defendants, Casey White is presumed innocent.

Chris Connolly

Lauderdale County District Attorney

Phone: 256-764-6351

chris@daconnolly.com

(Lauderdale County District Attorney's Office)

IN THE CIRCUIT COURT OF LAUDERDALE COUNTY, ALABAMA

STATE OF ALABAMA
Plaintiff,

CASE NOS: CC-20-511
DA-15-824

vs.

CASEY COLE WHITE

Defendant,

MOTION TO NOLLE PROSS

The State hereby moves to nolle pross this case, with leave to reinstate. The following is submitted in support of this motion:

1. The Defendant is serving a life sentence in the Alabama Department of Corrections (See 41-CC-642 along with sentences totaling 75 years in the Alabama Department of Corrections (See 41-CC-16-177). He will not be eligible for parole consideration until 2081.

2. The trial of this case will require the expenditure of significant State resources.

3. Investigators are continuing to actively investigate this case, including but not limited to the potential involvement of other people in the murder of Connie Ridgeway.

4. This motion is being made after consultation with investigators and discussion with Ms. Ridgeway's children, Austin and Cameron Williams, who support the filing of this motion.

Based on the foregoing, the State moves the court to nolle pross this case, with leave to reinstate.

Respectfully submitted, this the 28 day of July 2023.

/s/Chris Connolly
CHRIS CONNOLLY
DISTRICT ATTORNEY
P. O. BOX 914
FLORENCE, ALABAMA 35631-0914
(256) 764-6351

CERTIFICATE OF SERVICE

I hereby certify that I have provided a copy of the foregoing Motion to Hon. Robert Tuten, Attorney for the Defendant, by e-file, on the 28 day of July 2023.

/s/Chris Connolly
CHRIS CONNOLLY
DISTRICT ATTORNEY

(Lauderdale County District Attorney's Office)

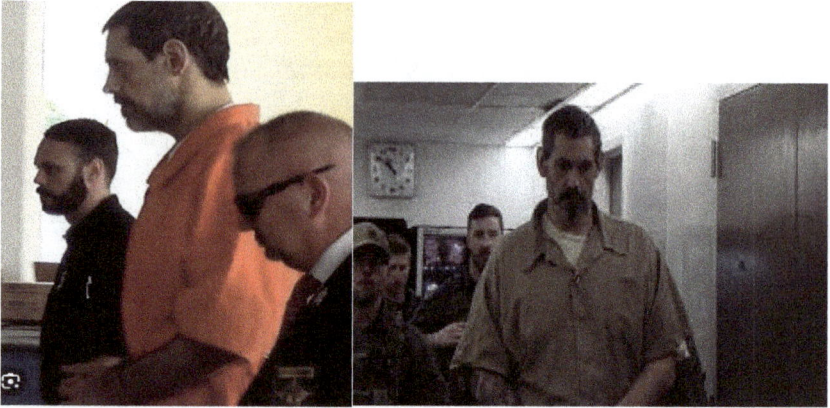

Left and above: Casey is escorted to court by Deputies for hearings after his capture.
Below: Sheriff Joe Hamilton, who replaced Sheriff Singleton in January 2023, escorts Casey to court for his sentencing on the escape charge. He was sentenced to life in prison.

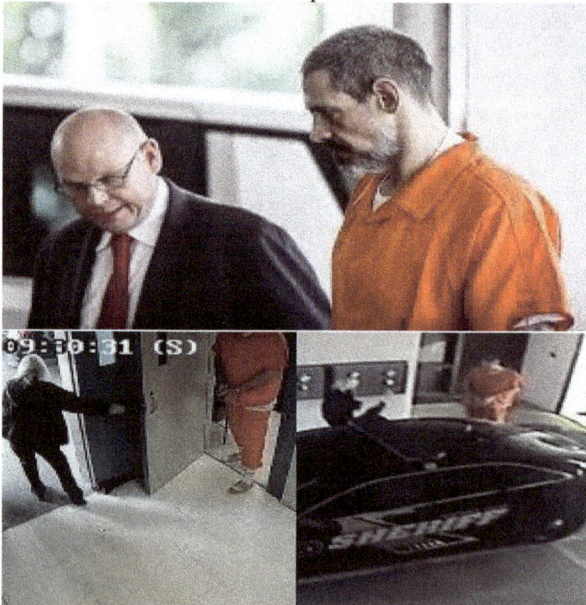

(Photos by Dan Busey/Times Daily)

CHAPTER 16

The Perfect Storm

The obvious question when something like this happens is: HOW? How in the world can someone, especially someone facing felony murder charges, just walk out of jail? Obviously, there's an explanation because it happened. The fact is there is no single factor that enabled Casey White to leave the Lauderdale County Detention Center on April 29, 2022. It was a combination of factors coming together much like the *perfect storm.*

There are three elements in the crime triangle that must be present for a crime to occur. If any one of the three elements is missing, then you cannot commit the crime. Those elements are: (1) a criminal; (2) a victim; and (3) an opportunity.

Crime Triangle

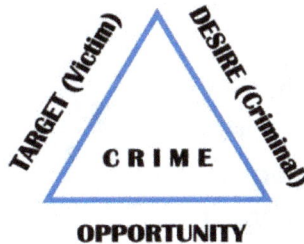

The criminal in this case, was Casey White. From the first day he reported to Donaldson Correctional Facility in 2019, he had one thing on his mind: escape! His mission in life was to get out of jail, something he desperately desired. I read many comments on social media stating that Casey didn't escape, that he was let out. Even though he literally *walked out* as opposed to *breaking out*, it is considered escape none-the-less. There has not been a "break-out" at the Lauderdale County Detention Center since 2016. Those escapes were due to design flaws in the facility that were finally addressed under my administration. With that said, he had to find an opportunity to execute an escape plan. That would be somewhat challenging given his circumstances. His best opportunity was to get inside help, which he did in Vicky White. He obviously, as I stated earlier, identified Vicky as a potential accomplice on his first incarceration in the facility. He saw something in her that convinced him he could persuade her (manipulate) to help him, and he played that to the hilt. She became his target.

Why was Vicky, the victim, selected as the target? There are several reasons why she was selected. She was the Assistant Administrator who literally had the keys to the door. There was no other employee who could possibly have pulled this off, who would have had the opportunity, other than the director himself.

To begin with, Vicky coordinated all inmate transport's and assisted with transports herself on a regular basis, therefore, it was not out of the ordinary for her to leave the facility with an inmate.

Photo of Vicky's Patrol Car.

(Rick Singleton)

She was the only one who received the list of inmates to be transported to court. It would have been very easy for her to add an inmate's name to that list without anyone's knowledge. She also assigned transport officers to the detail. She was the one to give the command to corrections officers inside the facility to prepare inmates for transport. Assigning these duties to a single employee, as we learned through this escape, were flaws in our procedures that were identified in a review after the escape. We had given too much authority and control over inmate transports to one person. That was addressed immediately to hopefully prevent a similar occurrence in the future by combining the two transport units, one at the detention center for local transports and one at the sheriff's office for prison transports and extraditions, into a single unit assigned out of the sheriff's office. The inmate court list is now sent to the sergeant over the unit, and he/she disseminates them to the transport team and detention center personnel for a system of checks and balances. Judges must now put any request for additional inmates to be brought before the court in writing, whereas before they would simply have a clerk make a phone call to the DC. Vicky also had charge of the facility. She made cell assignments and determined when and where inmates were to be moved.

On a personal level, in addition to her authority within the walls of the detention center, Vicky was a very caring person. She tried to make a difference in the lives of the inmates when and how she could. She was seen as a "mother figure" by many employees as well as inmates. This is something Casey probably picked up on very quickly.

Vicky had been divorced for nearly twenty years and had had only one romantic relationship since the divorce. She had gotten engaged, but that relationship ended in tragedy when her fiancée was killed in an accident. She had a very limited social life outside of work and would have been vulnerable when it came to attention from a man. Corrections officers are under a tremendous amount of stress and, as an administrator, that stress is multiplied tenfold. Burnout can take its toll both mentally and physically, resulting in discontent with the job and/or a desire to move on. These factors would have made Vicky an easy target, and Casey had all the time he needed to assess his situation and make his move.

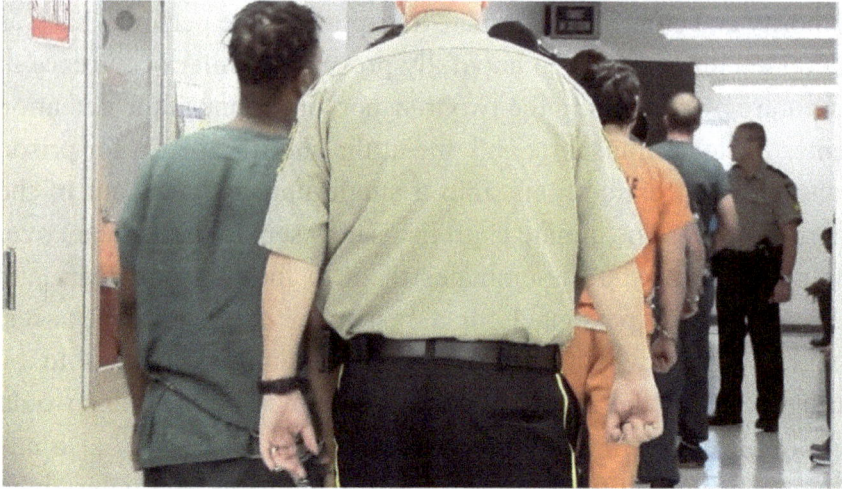
Corrections Deputies escort inmates to court at the Lauderdale County Courthouse.

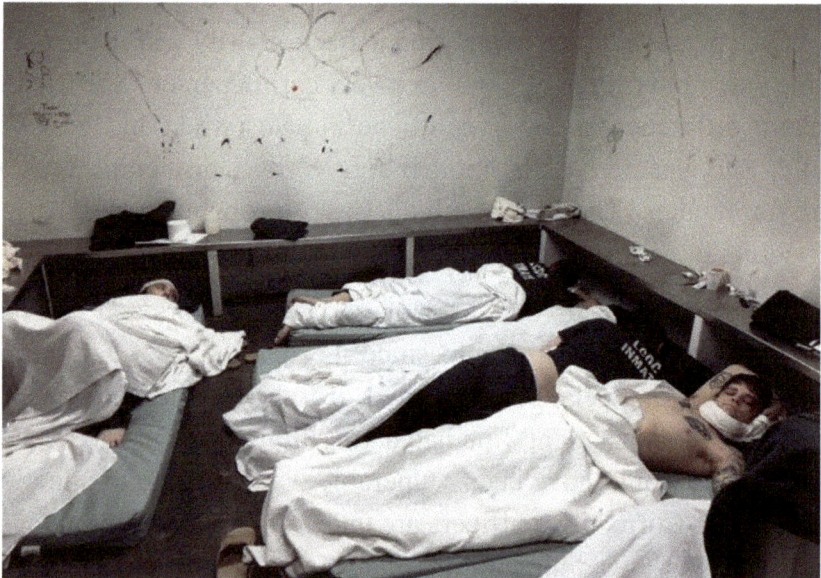
(Photo by Dan Busey/Times Daily)
Inmates sleeping on the floor in a holding cell. Peak inmate population in the 256-bed facility was 408 inmates with 152 of them sleeping on the floor.
(Lauderdale County Sheriff's Office)

As I said, the third element of a successful crime is opportunity. Many of the factors that made Vicky a target also presented the perfect opportunity for her to make this happen. The only other person who could have possibly had the opportunity to pull this off was the director himself and that is because of their positional power. They literally had the keys to the jail. With the duties and responsibilities of her position, along with the power and authority she had over the DC, she was certainly in the position, and had the opportunity, to pull this off.

So, with the offender, target, and opportunity identified, it was simply a matter of putting a plan together. I said earlier it was like a perfect storm. Vicky's situation and position were certainly factors in pulling this off, but there were other factors as well.

Crowding has been an issue at the detention center since the state legislature passed a prison reform bill in 2015. The new law resulted in many inmates serving their time in the local county jails across the state. The Lauderdale County Detention Center was opened in 1996 and designed to house 150 inmates. The original design included four cell blocks with eight isolation cells each. By the early 2,000's, the inmate population had outgrown the facility, so the isolation cells were converted into two-man cells, making a total of 203 beds. A woman's dorm was added in 2018, adding another 53 beds for a total of 256. In 2022, the average daily population was around 330, with a peak inmate population of 408. With no single inmate isolation cells in the facility, it was impossible to separate Casey White, and other serious offenders, from the population as they should have been. There's no question Casey White should have been under 24/7 surveillance.

Staffing was another factor. With a total allotment of 42 corrections deputies, on April 29th we had 31 on staff. Every shift was shorthanded. With four deputies tied up on transports, there was a skeleton crew at the DC when Vicky and Casey left the building. In fact, there were only two COs working the halls in the main facility when they left.

Certainly, our policies and procedures were a factor. There's no question Vicky violated policy on April 29th, specifically the one requiring two sworn deputies to escort inmates like Casey White, but it was the job description of the Assistant Director of Operations, more so the assignment of duties and responsibilities in the job description, that gave her so much authority and control over the inmates, especially the transports. If the changes we made after the 29th had been in place on that day, it would have been much more difficult, if not impossible, for her to have pulled this off.

So, the perfect storm?

1. An offender who desperately wants out of jail.

2. A corrections officer who is vulnerable.

3. A job description that gives that officer too much authority and control over inmates.

4. A facility that prohibited the proper incarceration of high-risk inmates.

5. A staffing shortage due to turnover leaving inexperienced officers who would not question the Assistant Director.

6. A knowledgeable employee who knew how to develop the perfect alibi by feigning illness so her absence would not be noticed for hours.

When these elements came together, an inmate serving a seventy-five-year sentence and awaiting trial for capital murder, was able to walk right out of the facility unchallenged.

View of front entrance and parking lot of the Lauderdale County Detention Center (Photo by Rick Singleton)
(Photo by Rick Singleton).

BLUE ALERT – EXTREME DANGER

Casey White

Vicky White

NAME: Casey White

INCIDENT DATE: 4/29/2022

AGE: 38

SEX: Male   RACE: White

HAIR: Gray   EYES: Hazel
HEIGHT: 6'6" WEIGHT: 252 Lbs.

CIRCUMSTANCES: Casey White is being sought in connection with a missing Lauderdale County Correctional Officer, Vicky Sue White.

If you see this person, immediately call 911 and provide authorities with as much information as possible, particularly regarding descriptions and direction of travel.

Blue Alert issued by ALEA. (Courtesy of ALEA)

CHAPTER 17

You Play the Hand You're Dealt

There's nothing in life that prepares you for the way you feel when you are betrayed by someone you have total confidence and trust in. Those of us who knew and worked with Vicky White ask ourselves till this day, "What in the world possessed her to do this?" An experienced veteran of corrections, she had seen this scenario play out many times over her career: a prisoner escapes by one means or another, they're on the run for a few hours or maybe a few days, but they always get caught. Always. She had to know deep down that they were not going to get away with this. She even left her insurance policy and will at her mother's house, where they would easily be found. Yet she went through with it anyway.

She had also obviously seen how inmates can manipulate corrections employees. As a supervisor and administrator in the detention center, she had been involved in numerous incidents where employees were caught bringing contraband into the facility, manipulated by inmates to do something they knew was not only wrong and against policy, but unlawful. As sheriff, I had implemented a zero- tolerance policy for employees bringing contraband into the jail and over the course of my tenure terminated and arrested four of our own for violating that policy. One of those employees was smuggling drugs into the facility in a bible. During interviews we stressed that policy to applicants and informed them of what the consequences would be if they violated it. We also told them to be prepared, that they would probably be tested on the first day of the job. Even with such stern warnings some employees allowed inmates to manipulate them, much like Vicky was manipulated by Casey White. With her background and experience, he was undoubtably a "master" manipulator.

To say I, and everyone who knew Vicky White, was blindsided by her actions would be an understatement. None of us would have imagined her doing something like this in our wildest dreams. In hindsight, I certainly learned a lot from this experience.

Vicky leads Casey White to the waiting patrol as they escape from the Lauderdale County Detention Center. (Lauderdale County Sheriff's Office)

First, *no corrections employee is immune from the influence of inmates*. If Vicky White could be manipulated to pull a stunt like this, anyone could be. It takes a special person to work in a jail or prison setting, and I have the utmost respect for the men and women in the corrections profession. Their job is challenging, stressful, and dangerous. They are exposed to threats and intimidation every day of their career. On top of that they are grossly underpaid. Every jail in the country struggles to keep employees for those reasons, and the turnover rate is astronomical. On April 29th, the day of the escape, we were eleven deputies short in the detention center, a full shift. That shortage of manpower was one of the factors that allowed this to happen in the first place, along with the inexperience of those who were working.

Second, *you may think you know someone, but you really don't*. There's no way you can know what's going through someone's mind. We hear a lot of talk about "red flags." They are always there, but most are only recognized through hindsight, after the fact. Vicky had been talking about retirement for several months. No big deal. We all talk about retirement, but while Vicky was vested in her retirement, she didn't have the years in, nor was she old enough to start drawing a check. In hindsight, that could have been a red flag, but no one thought anything about it at the time. Some people retire early. She was single with no children and could have had substantial savings. No one knew. Another potential red flag was having her co-worker pick her up at Academy Sports two days before the escape. The employee said she thought it was a little "weird," but dismissed it as, "Oh well." The point being that we're all human, and we normally aren't suspicious of the actions and decisions of the people we think we know unless it's something extraordinary in their behavior.

Third, the best policy in the world can't prevent the misconduct of an employee any more than a law can prevent crime. Theres no question our policy was lacking when it came to transporting inmates. After all, we amended our own policy after Casey White had planned an escape from LCDC in 2020, and we amended it again after this incident. The biggest flaw in our policy was having a transport team assigned to work out of the detention center under the supervision of detention center staff. That was absolutely on me as sheriff. As Assistant Director

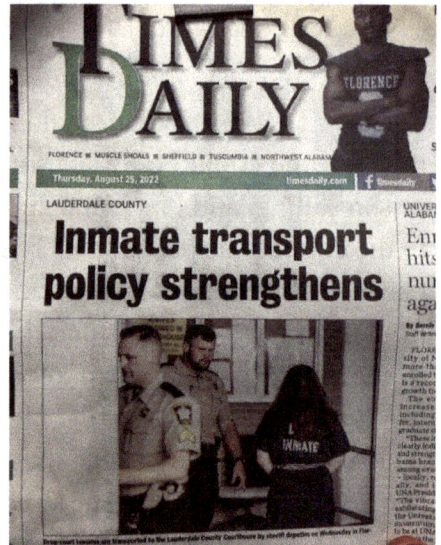

(Courtesy of Times Daily)

of Operations, I had allowed Vicky White to have total control over the removal and transportation of inmates from the detention center,

I had unwittingly put her in a position to pull the escape off without realizing it because I trusted her and never would have thought of her pulling such a stunt. My trust was misplaced because I thought I knew her. With that said, on Friday April 29th, 2022, I was dealt a hand that I had to deal with. Vicky White, the only person in a position and with the authority to pull such an event off (other than the director himself), led Casey White out the door of the Lauderdale County Detention Center. As sheriff, I was responsible for the custody and control of inmates, including Casey White, therefore the escape and getting Casey White back behind bars was on me. It was one of, if not the most challenging event in my fifty-year career.

Obviously, a local county sheriff's office doesn't have the resources nor the ability to conduct a nation-wide manhunt. My experience was the best thing I had going for me, and I knew immediately to get the United States Marshalls Fugitive Task Force involved. They have always had an outstanding reputation when it comes to tracking down fugitives, and they certainly lived up to that reputation in the case of Casey White. Taking advantage of her knowledge of the system, Vicky and Casey managed to go a full week before my investigators and the marshals picked up their trail. Once that happened, the pair was apprehended within 72 hours.

In my opinion, the national media also played a major role in this case by keeping the public informed and up to date on what was going on. Photos of Vicky and Casey were plastered all over the news, on television, in newspapers, and on social media. I'm convinced that was what forced them to check into the motel in Evansville, Indiana where they had planned to stay for two weeks. And, as I repeatedly stated during interviews, it was ultimately tips from the public that led to their capture, along with old-fashioned "boots on the ground" police work on the part of investigators.

In conclusion, as the old saying goes, "It is what it is!" Were there things I could have done as sheriff to prevent this from happening in the first place? Absolutely. Hindsight is always 20/20.

Media coverage played a vital role in getting the public's help in locating Casey and Vicky White. (Dan Busey/Times Daily)

Should I have seen this coming. It's easy to say that I should have when Monday morning quarterbacking. Did I see it coming? Not in the wildest stretch of my imagination. The one thing I am most grateful for is that no law enforcement officer or member of the public was hurt while Vicky and Casey were on the run or when they were apprehended. I thank God for placing a hedge of protection around any and everyone who had contact with them over the course of those eleven days.

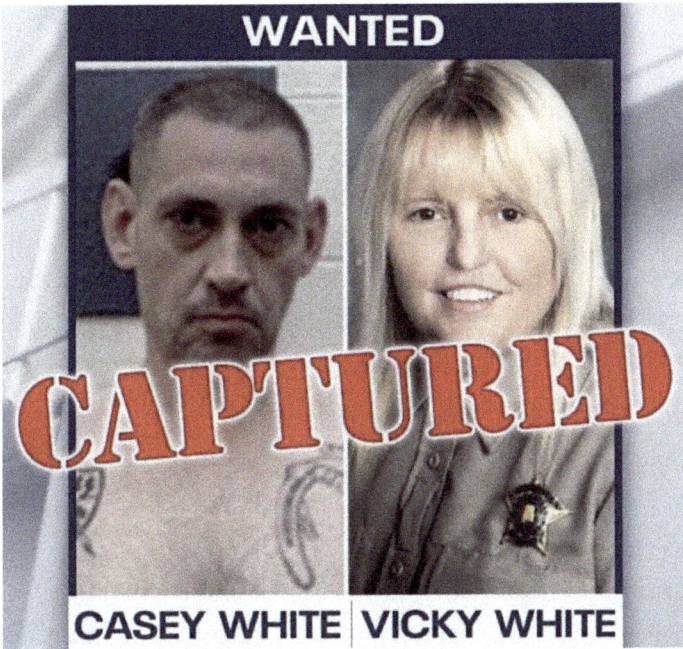

(United States Marshals Service)

CHAPTER 18

Life After the Capture

I've heard locals say they just wish this would end, but in my opinion it hasn't and probably never will. This is, without a doubt the most significant historical law enforcement event that has ever happened in Lauderdale County Alabama. Not only did it garner national attention, but international news outlets covered the case from beginning to end.

Within six months, the first of at least two movies came out on TUBI, a streaming service of Fox, called *"Prisoner of Love."* The second movie, *"Bad Romance: The Vicky White Story,"* premiered on Lifetime in October 2023. At least three documentaries on the escape were filmed for major productions including 20/20 and Netflix. In addition to this book documenting my own experiences as the sheriff responsible for seeing that Casey White was captured and sent back to prison, at least one other author, who specializes in true crime novels, is writing a book on the case as well.

News crews also continue to cover the case as new developments present themselves. Casey's return to court to enter his plea on the escape, the District Attorney deciding to suspend the charges for the murder of Connie Ridgeway, and the sentencing for the escape were all covered by local as well as national news stations.

Law enforcement and the community also continue to be fascinated by the case. The sheriff of Morgan County Alabama, Sheriff Ron Puckett, asked that I come over and speak to his supervisors and commanders about the case and what we learned from the experience. I've also spoken at statewide law enforcement conferences and civic clubs like the Rotary Club in Whitehouse, Tennessee.

Billy Risner, former co-worker and long-time friend of Vicky's, interviews with Angie Dorr of Dan Abroms Productions for a documentary. (Photo by Rick Singleton)

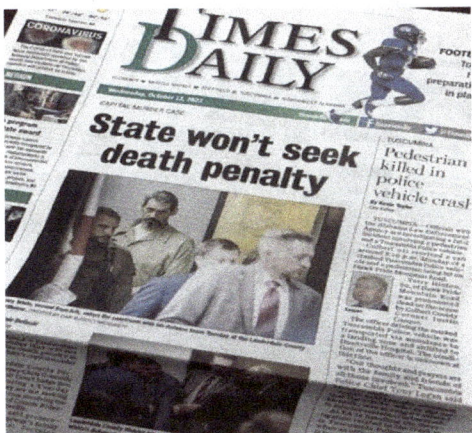

Courtesy of Times Daily

While it's hard to see the good in a situation like this, some positive things do come from such experiences. I got to know several of the national media personalities and especially those who work behind the scenes, producers, cameramen, etc.

One of the most courteous and genuine people I spoke with during the dozens of interviews I did was Don Lemon who, at the time, was a news anchor for CNN. The first night I appeared on his program the producer asked me to hold the phone after the interview was over. They went to a commercial break, and Mr. Lemon came on the phone. He thanked me for my time and expressed genuine concern about the situation, especially for Vicky. I appeared on his program two more times, and each time we had very candid discussions after the interview. The one thing he said that I vividly remember was, "I think she really loved him."

Sheriff Singleton addresses the supervisors and commanders of the Morgan County Sheriff's Office about the escape in November 2022. (Courtesy of MCSO)

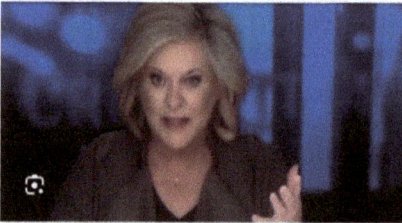

Escaped Alabama inmate reportedly dressed as 'little...   Watch

Uploaded: May 7, 2022
Fox Nation host and former prosecutor Nancy Grace gives an eerie premonition as to how the manhunt will end for corrections officer Vicky White and inmate Casey White.

Nancy Grace covered the escape from early on in the investigation and reached out more than once with words of support and encouragement. (Courtesy of Nancy Grace)

Nancy Grace was another news personality who reached out to me more than once to follow up with the case, especially as there were new developments. She, as always, had a unique insight as to what was going on and was a delight to work with. I'll never forget the messages of support and encouragement she sent me while the manhunt was actively in progress.

One man who has become a lifetime friend is James Stinson. A blogger came by my office one day, and they had just left Evansville, where they spoke with James. They had his phone number and asked if I would speak with him if they called. I, of course, said I would, and he mentioned that he would like to come down someday and meet with me. I told him I'd buy his lunch if he made the trip down. A few weeks later, he came in with his brother and a local reporter from Evansville, El'Agance Shemwell (Ellie), whom I liked right away. We

David Stinson (L) and James Stinson (R) Visit Sheriff Singleton on one of several trips they made to Florence Alabama. (Courtesy of ElAgance Shemwell)

talked for a while, took some photos, and then I kept my promise and bought their lunch. James made several trips back to Florence to attend various hearings and court proceedings relative to the case. I, in turn, made a trip to Evansville, where he showed me various points of interest including the motel where Vicky and Casey were staying and where the pursuit ended.

Throughout this ordeal, and until this day, it seems everyone has their opinion of Vicky White. To many, she is nothing more than a criminal herself, someone who put others' lives in jeopardy for selfish motives. To others, she was a victim of Casey's cunning manipulation, an exemplary employee who was vulnerable and, in a moment of weakness, let her emotions get the best of her. Both positions have valid points. But how about those of us who really knew her, who worked with her for all those years? How do we feel?

James Stinson and El'Agance Shemwell talk with Sheriff Singleton in his office during a visit after the capture of Vicky and Casey White. (Photo courtesy of WEVV TV)

Obviously, I can only speak for myself. I want you to know up front that I absolutely hate what Vicky did. I would give anything if April 29th, 2022, had never happened, but it did, and while I hate what she did, I cannot hate Vicky.

Vicky was a dedicated and loyal coworker who could be depended on for whatever task she was given. I considered her a friend, not in the sense that we socialized together, but in the sense that I would have been there for her if she ever needed anything, and I feel certain that she would have done the same for me. I was told by investigators that Casey told them she had wanted to call me. I'm not sure exactly when and certainly don't know why. I can only speculate, but based on the relationship we had in the past, I am convinced she wanted to apologize for putting me, her coworkers, and our department through this, because THAT is the Vicky I knew, the Vicky we all worked with for so long.

In closing, I'm reminded of a story in the bible about a woman who was brought before Jesus for him to judge. She had committed adultery, and in accordance with the law of Moses she was to be stoned to death. The Pharisees asked Jesus his thoughts on the subject. His response: "Let he who is without sin cast the first stone." No one cast a stone and they all left. Jesus then told the woman she was forgiven and to "go and sin no more". As a Christian, I am compelled to show the love and compassion towards Vicky that Jesus showed this woman.

www.ingramcontent.com/pod-product-compliance
Lightning Source LLC
Chambersburg PA
CBHW060245030426
42335CB00014B/1601